PENGUIN BOOKS

HORRIBLE WORDS

Rebecca Gowers is the author of *The Swamp of Death*, shortlisted for the CWA non-fiction Golden Dagger Award, and of two novels, *When to Walk* and *The Twisted Heart*, both longlisted for the Orange Prize. She is also the most recent editor of *Plain Words*, the classic guide to the use of English by her great-grandfather Sir Ernest Gowers.

Horrible Words

A Guide to the Misuse of English

Rebecca Gowers

PENGUIN BOOKS

PENGUIN BOOKS

UK | USA | Canada | Ireland | Australia
India | New Zealand | South Africa

Penguin Books is part of the Penguin Random House group of companies
whose addresses can be found at global.penguinrandomhouse.com.

First published by Particular Books 2016
Published in Penguin Books 2017
001

Set in 10.5pt/13.5 Adobe Caslon Pro
Typeset by Jouve (UK), Milton Keynes
Printed in Great Britain by Clays Ltd, St Ives plc

A CIP catalogue record for this book is available from the British Library

ISBN: 978–0–141–97897–0

www.greenpenguin.co.uk

MIX
Paper from
responsible sources
FSC® C018179

Penguin Random House is committed to a
sustainable future for our business, our readers
and our planet. This book is made from Forest
Stewardship Council® certified paper.

CONTENTS

PART I

ON HORRIBLE WORDS: *monsters and barbarities*   3

1 SLIPSLOPS: *poultry interest rates*   7

2 FOLK ETYMOLOGIES: *harbringer*   18

3 CONVERSION; VERBIFYING: *a creative, to routine*   27

4 BACK-FORMATIONS; IZE-MANIA: *to evolute, to reliabilize*   37

5 THE PAST TENSE: *snuck*   44

6 TRANSITING TRANSITIVITY: *coincide it*   50

7 PHRASAL VERBS: *to understand up*   54

8 COMPOUNDS IN GENERAL: *to rage-quit*   61

9 PARTICULAR COMPOUNDS: *to downstream*   67

10 PORTMANTEAU WORDS; MERGING; METANALYSIS: *webinar, alright, nother*   73

11 SYNCOPE; MUMBLING; MANGLING: *deteriate, euw, infatic*   82

12 BABY TALK: *ouchie*   89

13 AFFIXES: *innuendous*   97

14 ABSTRACT NOUNS: *operationalisation*   105

15 NEGATIVES; OPPOSITES: *disinterested, outro*   113

16 DOUBLE NEGATIVES: *irregardless*   122

17 WORD INFLATION: *precautious*   129

18 IMPRECISION: *monumentous*   138

PART II

ON REGISTER: *viscera, vitals and pluck*   149

19 FANCY LANGUAGE: *clinquant ansation*   155

20 MONOSYLLABLES: *zap*   163

21 BOVRILISATION: *ikr*   172

22 MACARONIC HOO-HA: *disploded yawps*   182

23 IN CONCLUSION: *bastards and syllables*   188

Acknowledgements   193

Index   195

PART I

'But when we look round on the vast multitude of writers who, to all seeming, deliberately aim at failure, who take every precaution in favour of failure that untutored inexperience can suggest, it becomes plain that education in ill-success, is really a popular want. In the following remarks some broad general principles, making disaster almost inevitable, will first be offered, and then special methods of failing in all special departments of letters will be ungrudgingly communicated.'

ANDREW LANG, *How to Fail in Literature*, 1890

ON HORRIBLE WORDS

monsters and barbarities

Under the letter H, *The Economist Style Guide* has an entry on what it calls 'horrible words'. With every appearance of judiciousness, it declares, 'Words that are horrible to one writer may not be horrible to another, but if you are a writer for whom no words are horrible, you would do well to take up some other activity'. Similar volumes on style go even further in anathematising certain words as 'non-words'.

The term *non-word* was first dreamt up by philosophical Victorians hoping to hint at something mysterious: 'By the word alone is the non-word revealed'; 'By giving Scripture a wrong sense ... men make God's Word become their own non-word', etc. However, *non-word* has long since jumped the bounds of lofty discourse and is now a word for a word that is not a word—rather as rebellious citizens under merciless political regimes are sometimes labelled 'non-persons'. Of course, a non-word is harder than a non-person to restrain, let alone to murder.* But there are those who try; and their influence can be traced in all the hedging found below:

> People feel – jargon word – empowered, they feel in charge of their destinies ...   (*Guardian*)

* For more on *verbicide*, see p. 136.

3

Thousands of men are receiving testosterone treatments funded by the HSE to combat the so-called 'manopause'. (*Sunday Times*)

We live a life of many dinners, many haircuts, many nappy changes. You can't narrate them all. You pick and choose. You (in the unlovely vernacular of our time) curate. (*Guardian*)

The story has, as the marketeers would put it, done a great job of enhancing the university's brand. (*Telegraph*)

... when any major figure from the art or entertainment world goes, so to speak, off-piste. (*Independent*)

Whose heart-cockles were not thoroughly warmed this week by the sweet letter that a head teacher wrote to her pupils and that went, as they say, 'viral'? (*The Times*)

... it's all a bit 'inspirational'—quote-unquote. (*Guardian*)

The actress has even gone so far as to delete all those old tweets—restarting her narrative, as it were. (*Washington Post*)

... a series of advertisements featuring, for want of a better word, 'real' people. (*Guardian*)

Read enough sentences of this kind, and it can start to seem a bit shabby the way their authors disavow the very words that, to all appearances, best suit their purpose.

Still, it is nothing new to express qualms about the odd 'barbarous vocable', as Coleridge put it, or 'paper-sore', A. P. Herbert's dismissive term.* Swift, in a letter of 1712 entitled *A Proposal for Correcting, Improving and Ascertaining the English Tongue*, wrote

---

* Coleridge was referring to the word *talented* (see his *Table-talk* for 8 July 1832). For no good reason, he thought that lack of an intermediary verb, to *talent*, made *talented* illegitimate. In *What a Word!*, 1935, Herbert, a politician

of there being 'many Words that deserve to be utterly thrown out of our Language'. A century and a half later, the American intellectual Richard Grant White would discuss at length what he called 'monsters' and 'words that are not words'.* Mostly, White noted, his 'words-no-words' were 'usurpers, interlopers, or vulgar pretenders'; but some he classed as 'deformed creatures'; while others, though 'legitimate enough in their pretensions', he considered 'oppressive, intolerable, useless'.

White was free to feel oppressed—naturally—if that was how it took him. But for him to say that the words that happened to oppress him were 'useless' was not wholly logical (logic being, he believed, immensely important). The monsters must have had their uses. Why else did he bother about them?

This question suggests itself now not least because people continue to be bothered by what they think of as lexical vulgarities, grotesqueries and abominations: the abuse is as immoderate today as it ever was. But is blanket contempt of this kind really good enough? Perhaps it is time to give our horrible words a little more thought.

---

and satirist, listed numerous neologisms that he, like *The Economist Style Guide* after him, found 'horrible'.
* *Words and their Uses*, 1870.

SLIPSLOPS

poultry interest rates

On 8 January 1788, Fanny Burney recorded in her diary that a certain Mr Bryant, entertaining her with 'good-humoured chit-chat', had recited 'a great number of comic slip-slops, of the first Lord Baltimore'. A 'slip-slop', she added, as though not previously aware of the term, was the accidental 'misuse of one word for another'.*

The label *slipslop* was being applied to this type of gaffe in homage to Mrs Slipslop,† a character from Henry Fielding's novel of 1742, *Joseph Andrews*. Mrs Slipslop mistakes *fragrant* for *flagrant*, *virulent* for *violent*, and speaks slightingly of the type of 'nasty' woman who is 'a Scandal to our Sect'. Byron liked this joke so much that he repeated it in a letter of 1813, referring to 'what Mrs. Slipslop terms the "frail sect"'. And in 1800, Matthew 'Monk' Lewis—a writer of ghost stories, himself haunted by charges of plagiarism—would shamelessly drop a revenant 'Mrs Slipslop' into a play of his own. Lewis's character is dreadfully prone to just the sort of error that marked her precursor, as when she says, 'it threw me into such a constellation, that I thought I should have conspired'. Yet, as Burney's remark shows, 'the

---

* By the lights of Richard Grant White, a 'usurper'.
† Before Fielding wrote *Joseph Andrews*, the word *slipslop* had generally been used to refer to a mixed dish or 'gallimaufry', or to dubious medicines.

slipslop' also came to stand as a concept in its own right. In an 1810 edition of *The European Magazine, and London Review*, there is a diatribe against parents who merely laugh when their children 'misconceive and misuse *words*'. Instead, the author declares in furious italics, any '*childish slipslop*' must be subject to '*parental reprehension*' to ward off permanent, awful, infantine '*oral deviations*'.

Modern readers may find themselves comparably dismayed by a reference to 'an identity spurned on by attachment and hatred',* or by the remark 'part of his remint will be to look at how points are scored' (*Daily Record*). And what of this, from a university counselling centre: 'A surface lack of interest in a subject may mask a deep seeded anxiety about future performance'? (Too true.) These sentences are bound to inspire charges of deviant word use, yet *spurning on* was perhaps being thought of as a form of reverse psychology; *reminting* conveys a not-irrelevant sense of renewal; and *deep-seeded* is if anything plainer than what it replaces. Meanwhile, could anyone really object to 'financial debacles such as banks getting bailed out whilst offering the bailers poultry interest rates'? This is too bonkers to be provoking; and even here there may be some redeeming thought of interest no better than chickenfeed, or of chickenshit returns.†

---

* P. F. Robinson, in *Large-Scale Victimisation as a Potential Source of Terrorist Activities*, Ewald and Turković (eds.), 2006, p. 279.

† NB Slipslops and puns can sometimes tread on each other's toes, but as with manslaughter and murder, they differ in the matter of intention: the switch contained in the phrase 'a deep-seeded anxiety' (*seeded* for *seated*) would no longer be a slipslop if a person were to say, deliberately, for its pathetic grain of humour, 'The Director at Kew has a deep-seeded love of plants'. And a pun, unlike a slipslop, can exist solely in the eye of the beholder: the solitary shopper laughing in the bread aisle of a Tesco or Marks and Spencer may have noticed—what both sell—the tragically self-abnegating 'Super Seeded Loaf'. Furthermore, where a slipslop requires some form of substitution, a

Word-switches of this kind have long been referred to by most English speakers, not as 'slipslops', but as 'malapropisms', after the garbled speech of Mrs Malaprop, a character in Richard Brinsley Sheridan's play of 1775, *The Rivals*. Famously, she speaks of 'an allegory on the banks of the Nile', 'the very pine-apple of politeness', and the like. But these substitutions, for *alligator* and *pinnacle*, are surreal, true out-and-outers, akin to the modern habit of mixing up *poignant* and *pertinent*.* A slipslop, by comparison, tends to make a modest amount of sense. As Leigh Hunt pointed out in an 1840 sketch of Sheridan, Mrs Malaprop is a 'caricature' of Mrs Slipslop—amusing, to be sure, but less believable.†

One can hold in mind this distinction between a slipslop and a malapropism without always being able to decide quite where the line should be drawn. In *Much Ado about Nothing*, Shakespeare's word-switching character Dogberry, in a typically foolish error, says, 'Comparisons are odorous'. Though *odorous* may be being misused here, it preserves the bad atmosphere of *odious*. In 1674, an anonymous pamphleteer slating Andrew Marvell chose to improve on Dogberry by saying, 'were not comparisons Odoriferous . . .', a version of the joke later falsely but repeatedly attributed to Mrs Slipslop.‡ In 1830, a reviewer for the *Edinburgh Literary Journal*, comparing comic annuals, rehearsed yet another

---

pun can play on variant meanings of a single word, as in: 'How does a cow show its approval? With a pat on the head'.

* 'Everything was so clear & poignant to my situation on that October day': Jan Baxter, *Ink Flow*, 2007, p. 32; 'an opportunity to make poignant to the industry the seriousness of this problem': *Computerworld*, 4 March 1991, p. 14.
† In 1841, the *Penny Cyclopedia of The Society for the Diffusion of Useful Knowledge* would call Mrs Malaprop a 'farcial exaggeration' of Mrs Slipslop.
‡ See E. S. Donno (ed.), *Andrew Marvell: The Critical Heritage*, 1978, p. 46. The pamphleteer's insults are so superb that we will not divert ourselves with the worry that, when he wrote this, *odoriferous* supposedly meant 'sweet-smelling': he adds shortly after, still trashing Marvell, 'it is enough to throw any man

mutation: 'In short, as Mrs. Malaprop says, "Caparisons are odor-iferous" …'. Again, the attribution is fanciful, but now we really are in the realm of the malapropism, *caparisons* being ornaments or armour for horses.

A broad term for swapping words in this fashion is 'catachresis'. Narrow the field, and you find that the slipslop, inasmuch as it is more plausible than a malapropism, is taken to be more insidi-ous as well. After all, an error of substitution would seem to pose a much greater threat of sticking where it makes a degree of sense. There are numerous examples currently in circulation. A 'steep learning *kerb*' for *curve* invokes an abrupt upward step;* '*parameter* fence' for *perimeter* maintains the sense of a boundary; to say 'in *cohorts* with' instead of *cahoots* still turns on a notion of fellowship; and 'free *reign*' for *rein* swaps the analogy of excess human power for that of an unconstrained horse. '*Right* of passage', it is true, appears to bypass all the fuss one might expect from a *rite*; and '*grit* to the mill', unlike *grist* (unground corn), would be a disaster for a loaf of bread. But 'chaise *lounge*' for *longue* explains exactly what the thing is for; '*superfluous* to requirement', though *surplus* to requirement, is absolutely clear; and there is even half an idea lurking in 'without further *due*': presumably, 'you've paid up; time to get on with it; no more *ado* required'. Being 'on the right *tact*' keeps to the general area of propriety that *tack* or 'course' implies. To say 'when all's *set* and done', rather than *said*, will often fully fit the bill. Likewise using 'in this *instant*' for *instance* may end

---

into a Fit of the Staggers to reflect upon your Confidence', and this must be the effect of the pamphleteer himself on his last few readers today.

* Perhaps the 'steep learning kerb', or in America, more contradictorily, 'curb', has been influenced by the idea of a 'step change', which in the second half of the twentieth century leaked from scientific writing into common parlance (or worse, according to John Humphrys in *Lost for Words*, 2004, into 'pretentious' common parlance).

up making about the same amount of sense, as in this gobbet from a volume dedicated to the psychoanalyst Lacan:

> The other example is that of the young homosexual when her father's gaze falls upon her as she is holding arms with her lady. In this instant, too, there is embarrassment followed soon afterward by a passage to the act in which she jumps over the parapet of the railway line.
>
> (Alexandre Stevens in *The Later Lacan*, Voruz and Wolf (eds.), 2007, p. 149)

These few examples are merely the start. Being 'in the *mist* of a storm' could be just as bad as being in its *midst*. When people speak of 'no love *loss*' between X and Y, the lost *lost* is hardly a loss at all. When demand or interest is said to have '*tailored* off', instead of *tailed*, an agreeable hint of exactitude enters in. And being '*streaks* ahead' adds the thrill of speed to the mere sense of distance conveyed by *streets*. Even the increasingly popular sign 'All Contributions *Greatly* Received' could be taken to impart a desirable flourish of gratitude.

Unlike malapropisms, which fall ridiculously wide of the mark, the slipslop or near miss tends to elicit much sniping from the public guardians of Good English. When *parameter* is used to mean *perimeter*, or *mitigate* to mean *militate*, staunch huffers and puffers can hardly contain themselves. In *The King's English*, 1997, Kingsley Amis calls the fellow who uses *infer* to mean *imply* a 'clot', and bashes T. S. Eliot for using *enormity* to mean *enormousness*: to the suitably informed, Amis declares, an 'enormity' suggests a dreadful transgression. Simon Heffer, in *Strictly English*, 2010, speaks of the 'obtuseness' of those who, even as they 'pretend to literacy', confuse *prevaricate* and *procrastinate*.* Will Self,

---

* Mr Heffer's work is subtitled '*The correct way to write . . . and why it matters*'.

meanwhile, in a newspaper review, decries another critic's 'howler'—what he calls the '"inchoate" for "incoherent" solecism'—scorning the misuse as 'hard to square' with the derided critic's 'quarter-century hacking away at the typeface'.*

A reader inclined to agree that the clot, the critic and T. S. Eliot were all disgracefully illiterate might nevertheless pause, mildly surprised, over another comment in this vein found in the work of Bill Bryson. He decides to offer guidance to those who, as he sees it, mistake being *celibate* for being *continent*, or 'chaste', by explaining that 'Celibacy does not, as is generally supposed, indicate abstinence from sexual relations. It means only to be unmarried . . .'.† The same reader might also pause for a moment when Mr Heffer, on *enormity*, declares that it is 'almost inevitably misused'. How does it make sense to say that a word 'generally supposed' to 'indicate' X does *not* 'indicate' X, or that one 'almost inevitably' used to mean Y is 'misused' when used to mean Y? Is it not true, the puzzled reader might wish to ask, that, in English, an error sufficiently widespread is an error no more?

---

* *Guardian*, 9 October 2013. (It seems equally likely that *inchoate*, or 'at a beginning stage', has become blearily confused with *chaotic*.) Not a year later, in the *BBC Magazine*, 31 August 2014, Mr Self would condemn those who 'don't like the ways in which our tongue is being shaped', calling the carpers 'small "c" conservatives, who would rather peer at meaning by the guttering candlelight of a Standard English frozen in time, than have it brightly illumined by the high-wattage of the living, changing language'. Quite so.
† See *Troublesome Words*, 1997. Mr Bryson, turning to the *Oxford English Dictionary* (the '*OED*'), might argue that it supports him by defining *celibacy* as simply 'The state of living unmarried'. But this is an unrevised Victorian entry, of which the *OED* still contains rather a number. (Its lexicographers slave to bring the work more thoroughly up to date.) And there is overwhelming evidence that this definition of *celibate* is no longer broad enough: 'the emphasis on sex as a leisure activity in consumer society allows people in celibate marriages to see their situation as something that can and should be remedied' (*Telegraph*); 'A Roman Catholic bishop who has been forced to resign after claims of a love affair with a parishioner says he wants to remain a priest, despite breaking his vows of celibacy' (*Sunday Times*).

Popular slipslops of the past provide an encouraging answer to this question. *Redound*, which from the late 1300s meant to 'surge' or 'swell over', has long since sheltered within the purlieus of a word coined a century or so later, *rebound*. Does anyone today give a fig about the lost, surging *redound*? Absolutely not. And what of *brothel*? In the fifteenth century this word was used to mean a prostitute, but soon after, it got mixed up with *bordel*, from the same Latin root as the Italian *bordello*, only to come out of the encounter with the meaning that we give it to this day. How many purists of our own time do we find expostulating about this switch? None. You may continue to have recourse to a 'brothel' just as you always expected to, with not the slightest fear of reproaches from them.

No, what matters to our purists is not the loss of a single word for a prostitute (there are so many others to choose from!), but the sight and sound of their own Good English being assaulted by those degenerates at the forefront of language change. When reading in a fashion column that 'the search for the perfect trouser was illusive' (*Guardian*), those trapped in Mr Self's 'guttering candlelight' must wince and sigh, as certain that the reporter's search was the opposite of *illusive* or 'illusory' as they are that it was in fact the 'perfect trouser', and not the search, that turned out to be *elusive*.* That particular quibble may sound like very small beer, but when another correspondent on the same paper explains that a dramatist wished his movie script about apartheid to convey 'the enormity of Mandela's achievement', the huffers and puffers will insist on understanding this use of *enormity* to imply, not awe, but crushing disapproval.† The same unhappy

---

* For more on the singular *trouser* (if you are keen) see pp. 144–5.
† *The Economist Style Guide* declares that *enormity* does not mean '*immensity*', but rather 'a *crime, sin* or *monstrous wickedness*'. (It happens that in its earliest uses, the word *enormous* meant both 'abnormal' and 'unusually huge'.)

effect is likely to be created by an advertisement for a rental property where the tag under a picture of the interior boasts, 'There's an enormity of expensively garnished living space', though at least here it would be possible for both interpretations of *enormity* to apply at once. Also discomfiting to some will be the words of the writer Mark Lawson, who, in an article on his own work, manages to invoke what our advisers would interpret as the megalomaniacal notion of *chartering*, 'hiring', whole planets, rather than the more graspable one of *charting* or 'mapping' them: 'I will proceed like an astronaut who, landing on a far, unchartered planet, tries to blink away what seems to be the reflection, in the window of his capsule, of a planted flag'.*

If we return to thinking about the fate of *redound* and *brothel*, it is surely reasonable to suppose that in years to come, pronouncers on lexical correctitude will have absorbed several of our current popular slipslops into their own version of Good English—a version they will quite possibly consider 'streaks' better than whatever parallel future English is destined to get on their nerves.† But this reasonable supposition about the future does not temper the grief of our own language guardians as they look about them today. Where a verbal switch is still in process, or indeed has only just begun, the most recent interpretation of an old word is bound to qualify in their minds as horrible: they will complain loudly and authoritatively that a useful fragment of our common tongue is at risk of losing its ideal meaning; they will despond as the

---

* *Guardian*, 6 September 2013.
† Many slipslops do, of course, simply fall out of use. In an essay in *The Olio*, 1792, entitled 'On slip-slopping, or the mis-application of words', Francis Grose lists several examples that are no longer in play, including the use of *successfully* for *successively*: 'I remember to have heard a landlord of an inn, descanting on the hardship of quartering soldiers, declare, that in the very town, in which we then were, half a dozen landlords of the neighbouring inn had all been successfully ruined'.

word starts to colonise the meaning of the decent other word for which it has been mistaken.

Still, griping about misuses is not pure misery for the gripers. Mark Twain had this to say about a piece of writing he considered 'hogwash': 'For five years I have preserved the following miracle of pointless imbecility and bathos, waiting to see if I could find anything in literature that was worse. But in vain. I have read it forty or fifty times, altogether, and with a steadily-increasing pleasurable disgust'.*

It is splendid to picture Twain enjoying himself like this forty or fifty times; but what if for you the 'pleasurable disgust' he mentions holds no great appeal? What if you are unbothered by the idea that English uses alter, and you blithely imagine that measuring today's verbal novelties against any losses they may force on the language is likely to result—if it even matters—in a net gain? Suppose all this fuss about solecisms and howlers leaves you thinking *phooey*: can you leave the field?

The answer to that is, categorically, no.

Sometime before he was killed in 1593, Christopher Marlowe, in one of his plays, wrote the following line, to be delivered with an arctic sneer: 'What doctrine call you this,' it went, 'Che sera, sera, / What wil be, shall be?'†

The same thought arises here.

Que sera sera, pal? *Uninterested* you may be; *disinterested*, never!‡ We all help to shape the language; it is just that in the battle for Good English waged ceaselessly by the gripers, your negligent approach puts you squarely with the forces of darkness. No need to enlist—you are doubtless misusing your words already; you

---

* *Galaxy*, June 1870. The piece in question began, 'A beautiful lady sat beneath a verandah overshadowed by clustering vines'.
† *The tragicall history of D. Faustus.*
‡ If you are in the least doubt about what this might mean, see p. 119.

probably chose sides long ago without even realising it. Well, if so, fair enough. And yet, *if* so, there is a question you really ought to be asking yourself. Why carry on in a state of partial ignorance, lobbing pebbles here and there, and being despised in return, when you could be disporting yourself with savage brilliance in the front lines?

If you were to put in a little effort, placing yourself in the vanguard of change, you would be sure to draw the fire of the gripers, and might even shield your yet more lackadaisical fellows in the process—those innocents silently done down by endless elitist opprobrium. We all know that a garish misuse, allowed to linger in the language, can come to seem less garish, or not garish in the slightest, just as the fairground colours on ancient Greek statues, washed away by the ages, reveal the gods and goddesses beneath to be coolly white. Shunt the battle lines of the language far enough ahead, and the humble old misuses that your confrères so resolutely favour will eventually be reclassified by your enemies as idiomatic; wonders to be celebrated; glorious and beautiful.

Should you set about such a campaign, you will find the armoury at your disposal to be huge: this guide explains the very best of its tanks, guns and bullets. But do not doubt that your fight will be bitter and long. You must steel yourself for what Swift called that 'Rudeness much practiced by Abhorrors',* after which, there could be no better way to begin than by running the *gambit*† of the misuses listed above. Indeed, just one of

---

* See *A Modest defence of Punning*, 1716.
† 'The studies that have been produced over the years have run the gambit in type, parameter, and result': Reginald J. Montgomery and William J. Majeski, *Corporate Investigations*, 2005, p. 130. You must decide for yourself what 'running the gambit' means. People have been running the *gamut* for three hundred years (a full span of musical notes), and the *gauntlet*, or 'glove', for even longer. Those who use the second phrase may be interested to learn that they are perpetuating a seventeenth-century misuse: the original term, derived

them would be enough to get you started. For it is a fact as remarkable as it is relevant to your new purpose that the griper has no mercy. Only resolve to prove your indifference to the exact limits of today's Good English, and a single slipslop will ruin your reputation for ever. As Thomas Gray had it in 1747, in his 'Ode on the Death of a Favourite Cat, Drowned in a Tub of Gold Fishes', a work inspired by the fate of Horace Walpole's cat Selima, 'Know, one false step is ne'er retrieved'—and so in the battle that faces you now. If you feel ready for the fray, are undaunted by your foes and have even the *poultriest* reserves of will to dedicate to the cause, then it is past time for your assault on the English language to begin.

---

from the Swedish, was *gantlope*, the running of which had nothing whatsoever to do with gloves. (For more on tiresome military punishments, see the tiresome *decimate*, pp. 139–40.)

2

FOLK ETYMOLOGIES

harbringer

You may have noticed in the previous chapter that it seemed helpful here and there to dip briefly into the histories of one or two words, or their 'etymologies'. And it is perhaps tempting to imagine that where there is a disagreement about what a word really means (whatever 'really means' means), an appeal to its origins, if they are known, will settle the matter. But what a shame it would be if that were true; and how lucky for you that it is *not* true. With your suddenly acquired purpose of challenging the defences set up around Good English, it can only be splendid news that the meaning of our words is above all a matter of custom.

When C. S. Lewis addressed this topic in 1960, in his book *Studies in Words*, he raised the excellent question of why anyone would ever bother to go round insisting on what a word did *not* mean. He noted that people display this kind of resistance only when a word has already picked up its new, supposedly wrong sense. The naysayers, he explained, were engaged in acts of 'tactical definition'.

In the following passage, Simon Heffer demonstrates perfectly what Lewis was on about: 'Many believe that for a person to be an *orphan* he [*sic*] must have neither parent alive. This is not so. An orphan is someone who has lost either parent; those who have lost both are double orphans'. What a pity Mr Heffer did not swish confidently past boring old *orphan* to seize on the word it replaced in the language: *stepchild*. Would he not have had more fun, and could he not have become even more indignant, if he had been exhorting us to unpick the etymology of *stepchild* instead, trying to make us understand it as it always used to be understood (some thousand years ago), when *stéop* meant bereaved? He could be fighting for printers to worry about 'widows and stepchildren'; for *orphanages* to become 'stepchildrenages', and so on.

He could be, but the truth is that the meanings of words can alter. Imagine the chatter when the first actor to play the lead in *Coriolanus* spoke of 'the Pibbles on the hungry beach'. Foh! In the standard English of the time, the word *beach* meant—pebbles. To the agitated griper of Shakespeare's day, Coriolanus might as well have been saying, 'the Pibbles on the hungry pibbles'. It is in part because of Shakespeare's own writing that the meaning of *beach* has shifted since, sparing our current gripers the need to gnash their teeth at this line.

Then again, the word *beach* happens to have no known origin, so that its meaning might be thought to be up for grabs. Where, by contrast, a word has unquestioned roots, there are those who pretend that these roots should be, in all senses, definitive (linguists call this the 'etymological fallacy'). This sort of thinking evidently underlies the declaration by Graham King, author of the *Collins Complete Writing Guide*, 2009, that it is a 'common misconception' that to *condone* means to 'allow or approve', when really it means to 'forgive'. Bill Bryson is with him on this, explaining that *condone* means 'forgive', and 'does not mean to approve or endorse'. It is plain that they have in mind *condone*'s Latin origin, more directly reflected in the English word *pardon*. However, their ruling would come as a shock to Rev. Albert Curry Winn, who in his work of 1990, *A Christian Primer*, boldly wrote that 'To forgive is not to condone'. To Messrs King and Bryson, the cleric's humdrum yet important observation must seem unfathomably philosophical. To the rest of us, it is presumably straightforward enough.

In a similar mood, Mr King writes that *pristine* does not mean 'spotlessly clean' but 'uncorrupted, original'. *The Economist Style Guide* agrees: *pristine* 'means *original* or *former*; it does not mean clean'. Mr Heffer likewise declares: 'It means original'. How so? Again, they are adhering to the word's Latin roots—the Latin *pristinus* means 'former' or 'ancient'. You can bet, however, that when the *Telegraph* newspaper—whose use of English Mr Heffer officially monitors—flags 'three steps to achieve a pristine lawn', it is explaining how to remove moss and clover from a neglected patch of grass, not proposing that its readers should abandon their morsels of sward to the most primitive of our native weeds.

If you have been using *condone* to mean 'approve', or *pristine* to mean 'clean' or 'sparkly', and if, despite the scales now being torn from your eyes, you secretly doubt that you will ever revise this habit, then you have all the evidence you need that usage is happy to trample etymology into the dust. Once again, if a 'common misconception' about the meaning of an English word is common enough, how the meaning came about will be irrelevant to whether or not it is, in practice, for now, correct. Nor are our advisers consistent about their etymological imperatives when it does not suit them to be. Mr Heffer, in his discussion of *orphan*, must have taken account of the origin of the word, yet cannot have found it convenient to note that in this case the Latin was against him. *Orphanus*, in its use by Saint Augustine, Venantius Fortunatus, et al., meant someone with neither parent alive.

But the fact that no English speaker uses every word of English in strict accord with its earliest known history does not mean that the general English speaker is impervious to the lure of etymological argument—a point perhaps best illustrated by instances of etymological reasoning being popularly misapplied. Changes in the use of the words *noisome* and *fruition*, for example, have arisen through false but mesmerising assumptions about how their parts fit together:

> Given a gun and told to bring his plans to fruition himself, would the meek Ross Ulbricht ever pull the trigger?   (*Independent*)

> Antonio Pappano conducted with his habitual gusto, and the show ended with a noisome mass rendition of the Sextet from *Lucia di Lammermoor*, some of the parts being doubled.   (*Telegraph*)

The eye can be deceived. The 'nois' in *noisome* is related, not to *noise*, as that of massed opera singers, but to the 'noy' in *annoy*. Many people do still use *noisome* to mean disgusting and repellent, but many do not. Similarly, *fruition*, by its etymology, should mean, not coming to full 'fruit', but rather 'enjoyment'—the Latin verb *frui* meaning *enjoy*. Three centuries ago, the poet Thomas Yalden could write, drearily yet plausibly, 'Fruition only cloys the appetite; / More does the conquest, than the prize delight'. Fruit-like ripeness appears to have overtaken the word completely since.

It is one thing for countless speakers to misconstrue a word's origin, and so to conspire to alter its meaning. It is quite another for this process to put so much pressure on a word that it actually changes form. Many people make such adaptations privately, for fun. Jane Austen, for example, used 'noonshine' as a pet substitute for *nuncheon*, the 'noon-drink' or midday snack of the time. (Browning, in 'The Pied Piper of Hamelin', writes cheerfully: 'So munch on, crunch on, take your nuncheon'.) But from time to time, a reworked word will gain a much wider currency.

When this happens, the dictionaries explain it as an example of 'folk etymology'. There is a notorious instance of this phenomenon built on the Old English word *shamefast*. By putting together *shame* and the idea of 'fastness'—the state of being caught or restrained, as in stead*fast*, *fast* friends, or being *fast* asleep—a word was created that initially meant 'caught by shame', often used in the virtuous senses of 'bashful' or 'modest'. *Shamefast* survived in this form for roughly six hundred years before becoming entangled with the idea of a person whose cheeks are flooded with a blush. It is true that this is a potent image: in the fourteenth-century poem *Sir Gawain and the Green Knight*, King Arthur is said to have been so humiliated by the ruthless green stranger that 'The blod schot for scham into his schyre* face'. At any rate, in the sixteenth century shame*fast* was suddenly up against shame*faced*; and perhaps there were some who decried the new, illiterate usage. But all in vain: the original form was done for, and duly disappeared.[†]

Another instance of a popular struggle after meaning can be traced in alterations to the expression *upside down*. It first appeared in the 1300s as *up-swa-doune*. Two centuries later, newer versions came into use, such as *vp set downe* and *upset downe*. But it was a yet more explanatory form, found in Coverdale's 1535 translation of the Bible—where a tent is turned *vpsyde downe* by a barley loaf—that would come to vanquish the rest.[‡]

The spelling *hiccough* for *hiccup* is a particularly odd example, given that we all still pronounce the word *hiccup*. We have had *hiccups* since the late sixteenth century; *hiccoughs*, from about a

---

* The word *schyre* meant 'shining'.
[†] Richard Chenevix Trench, Archbishop of Dublin, was still complaining about this in 1855, in his book *Synonyms of the New Testament*. To use *shamefaced* was, he said, 'to allow all the meaning and force of the word to run to the surface, to leave us ethically a far inferior word'.
[‡] In *Write it Right: A Handbook of Literary Faults*, 1909, Ambrose Bierce (best known now for his *Devil's Dictionary*) writes snippily of *head over heels*, 'A transposition of words hardly less surprising than (to the person most concerned) the mischance that it fails to describe. What is meant is heels over head'.

hundred years after that. An out-of-date *OED* entry, failing to acknowledge the long history of the later spelling, contains the stern judgement that *hiccough* 'ought to be abandoned as a mere error'. Yet whoever wrote its much more recent entry on *miniscule* was perfectly prepared to accept the popularity of this word. Not so the gripers, however. The original form *minuscule* is 'frequently misspelled', notes Mr Bryson. It is one of the 'most troublesome' challenges to spelling, writes Mr Heffer. In this instance, it would seem to be the ear that has misconstrued the original word, not the eye. Translated on to the page, however, the war over *minuscule* and *miniscule* hinges on whether you understand the word to be *minus* plus the diminutive suffix -*cule*, as in *molecule*, or *mini-* attached to 'scule'—meaning who knows quite what. (Those who write of *groupuscules*—political splinter groups—might be able to explain.)

Another word currently under pressure of this kind is *sacrilegious*, an adjective derived from the term *sacrilege*, but commonly now spelled 'sacreligious'* by those who wish to invoke some idea of religion: '. . . train tracks of diminishing width seems indecent, almost sacreligious . . .' (*Independent*). Meanwhile, 'commeasurate' is starting to be used for *commensurate*: 'O'Dell's attorneys attempted to get DNA analysis of the semen in the case commeasurate with scientific advances of the times'.† (It happens that *measure*, no less than *commensurate*, derives from the Latin verb *mensurare*.) Yet another word under threat of this sort of change is *remuneration*, 'pay'. Many people feel compelled to plant within it an echo of *numerals* or *enumerate*, not caring that *munus*, from

---

* If *sacrilegious* is *sacrilege* plus the suffix -*ous*, meaning 'full of', then in the variant form 'sac' plus *religious*, the question arises of what 'sac' is supposed to suggest. Perhaps it does convey something of the negative, as in the 'sack' of Rome.

† Richard A. Stack, *Grave Injustice*, 2013, p. 71.

which the component 'mun' is derived, is the Latin for a gift (as in *munificent*):

> It had already been criticised for offering free health insurance to a small number of senior staff as part of their renumeration. (*Telegraph*)

> ... do we need to introduce public sector renumeration committees to prune fat cat salaries? (*Guardian*)

> ... despite a growing controversy over the size of the payout it had 'no serious issues' with BP's renumeration policy. (*The Times*)

To those who still use the word *remuneration*, this writing will sound dismally untutored, though the earliest example of the switch cited by the *OED* is from 1572: 'the godly are afflicted without anye renumeration'.* All the same, it is not beyond imagining that our descendants will properly be 'renumerated' for their labours, with nary a purist eyebrow raised.

Perhaps even more offensive to the griper than *commeasurate* or *renumeration* will be the word *harbringer*: 'Edades is without question the harbringer of the new grammar to the land'; 'Callaghan so refined the political mechanism of former French operatives that many believed him the harbringer of a new age'; 'Non-violence is the harbringer of justice all round'.† What is this? The form *harbringer* is itself a descendant of the twelfth-century *herbergere*—originally a provider of lodgings—and is a word whose current meaning (of a sign of something greater to come)

---

* The Anglo-Norman 'remuneracyoun' dates from around 1400.
† Manuel D. Duldulao, *Contemporary Philippine Art: From the Fifties to the Seventies*, 1972, p. 15; Kenneth Mason, *African Americans and Race Relations in San Antonio, Texas, 1867–1937*, 1998, p. 111; M. G. Chitkara, *Converts do not make a Nation*, 1998, p. 348.

was arrived at only after it had started to be used to denote a person sent scouting ahead to find lodgings or camping grounds for a party of followers, knights, an army. The word *herbergere* mutated into *harbinger* on the same model as the word *passenger* (which originally meant 'ferryman'). It has had the forms *herbegeour*, *harbesher*, *harbiger*. One might wonder whether, with so much muddle behind it, the recent jump to *harbringer* is really such a crime.

It is not inevitable that *sacreligious* will write *sacrilegious* out of the language, nor that *renumeration*, now 450 years into its campaign, will ultimately kill off *remuneration*. Sometimes a mutation simply goes away again. In the late seventeenth century, the word *honeymonth* jostled competitively with the older *honeymoon*. The new form interpreted the 'moon' in *honeymoon* as implying a month's span, whereas what it had originally conveyed was the quality of being—as the moon is—changeable: how long two people might continue to like each other after marriage had been deemed hard to predict (it certainly is). And we now know that it was the open-ended interpretation—and the original form of the word—that would come to prevail, as when we speak today of a new government's enjoying a 'honeymoon period' with the voters.* Just as *honeymonth* fell right out of use, so too did the folk interpretation *wretchless*. In his dictionary of 1755, Samuel Johnson writes accusingly, 'This is, by I know not whose corruption, written for *reckless*'. The *OED* cites many examples, including the following by the Irish bishop George Rust, who wrote in 1661 of people 'wretchless and insensible of all wholesome

---

* Not that we ought to do this, according to *The Economist Style Guide*, which lists *honeymoon period* as a cliché that will 'numb' the reader's brain. Ambrose Bierce was still, in 1909, muttering about what he believed to be the correct meaning of *honeymoon*: 'Moon here means month, so it is incorrect to say, "a week's honeymoon," or, "Their honeymoon lasted a year"'.

counsels'. But at just the time of Johnson's verdict, use of *wretchless* began to decline, and today it has vanished entirely.

Let us assume that, from a griper's perspective, you too—with your desire to enlarge the scope of Good English—appear 'wretchless and insensible of all wholesome counsels'. It may not be within the compass of your abilities to dream up a new etymological botch job worthy of the examples listed above; and if so, sad as that is, never mind. You could nevertheless set about promoting any words you encounter whose origins are already being overwritten. Adopt one or two of these—so powerfully offensive to purist sensibilities—and you are bound to be dismissed by your foes as susceptible and weak. Yet they will also fear you as a lexical *harbringer* of doom.

3

CONVERSION; VERBIFYING

a creative, to routine

We have seen that a word can have more than one meaning. In the pun about the cow showing its approval with a pat on the head, the word *pat* refers either to a mild physical gesture or to a giant cake of ordure. And though it happens that in both these cases *pat* is deployed as a noun, a single word may also be put to more than one grammatical use: *pat*, for example, is, among other things, a verb as well. A widely cited humorous line that depends on this great flexibility in the language is: 'Time flies like an arrow. Fruit flies like a banana'. How you read the phrase 'fruit flies like a banana' is determined by the grammatical category you ascribe to the words *fruit*, *flies* and *like*; *flies*, for instance, can be read either as a verb—as in, 'it flies through the air', or as a noun—'those pesky buzzing flies'.*

The earliest surviving examples in English of uses of the word *fly* show it employed in both capacities. It occurs as a noun, the insect, in the *Lindisfarne Gospels*, and in *Beowulf*, as a verb, where a naked, flame-wreathed dragon 'flies' through the night. These two texts appear to be of much the same date; but often in

---

* On 18 August 1969, subscribers to *Screw* magazine had it patiently explained to them that 'fruit fly' was a variant term for a *fag hag* or *faggot's moll*, i.e. a woman who seeks out the company of homosexual men. Perhaps the joke had more layers to it than is commonly supposed.

English a word will start life as one class of word, say a noun, and only later—perhaps much later—begin to be used as another, say a verb, in a process linguists call 'word-class conversion'. Sticking for a moment with animals, the nouns *fox*, *ape*, *badger*, *fish* and *dog* took years, and in some cases centuries, to become verbs as well (to *fox*, to *ape*, to *badger*, to *fish*, to *dog*). Or take the word *cloud*. This too started out—in the ninth century—as a noun. It first meant a pile of rocks or a hill (*cloud* is etymologically related to both *clod* and *clot*). Then around 1300, clouds lifted off the ground to become heaps in the sky—since when the noun has always meant what we mean by it now. But it was not until the sixteenth century that *cloud* was also converted into a verb, meaning to 'darken' or 'obscure'. Shakespeare took the noun *blanket*, then three centuries old, and turned it into a verb in *King Lear*: 'My face I'll grime with filth, / Blanket my loins'. The word *fund*, a noun from the seventeenth century, became a verb a century later, as in this remark from 1785: 'they will fund the debt of one country and destroy the trade of another'*—and so it goes on. Words are converted from verbs to nouns, too. For instance, the verb to *walk* came before the noun *walk*, as in 'Let's go for a walk'; and the verb to *think* came before the noun *think*, as in 'I'll have a little think about it'. In fact, converting in both directions is commonplace.

So far, so good, you may be saying to yourself—though if you are, you would be wrong. John Humphrys, in *Lost for Words*, writes that, in English, 'verbs can refresh a sentence any time they are needed—but not if they earned their crust as nouns in an earlier life'. He can have had no idea when he said this of the apocalypse he was wishing on the language. More specifically, Kingsley Amis listed the use of *fund* as a verb among what he called 'easily

---

* See the Irish *Parliamentary Register* for 12 August 1785.

avoidable blemishes', apparently in the belief that it was a recent example of conversion. Martin Amis later concluded that his father's view in this had been fogeyish—but immediately described another 'blemish' on his father's list, the verb to *critique*, as genuinely 'regrettable'.* *The Economist Style Guide* almost pettishly agrees: '*critique* is a noun. If you want a verb, try *criticise*'.

You may be wondering what exactly the problem is here. Gripers cling to the idea that some words, or some uses of words, can be written off as horrible mostly because they are new, and therefore, by implication, redundant (nobody needed them before). Leaving aside the question of whether or not any part of this argument is valid, it is worth observing that lack of an ear for such things, and the will to check in a dictionary, means that those who shoot this line often mistake the age of what it is they are wishing to abolish.† No doubt there are entire armies of 'regretters' who would condemn as repulsive modern business-speak the verbs to *message*, *dialogue*, *routine*, *conference*, and so on. Yet, as the *OED* shows, these words were all first converted from nouns to verbs either decades or centuries ago. To *conference* dates from 1846 and would be used by Thomas

---

* See *The King's English* in the 2011 edition introduced by Martin Amis. The Amises fail to distinguish between the use of *critique* to mean 'criticise' and to mean 'evaluate'. To them, this nicety may have been irrelevant.

† Arguing against a word you dislike on the grounds that it is new, or newish, only to discover that it has a long history and is enjoying a renaissance, is a pitfall so common that it inspired the linguist Arnold Zwicky to coin the term the 'recency illusion'. (NB The word *recency* is itself a good four hundred years old, in case you were wondering; while *critique* as a verb is even older than the verb form of *fund*.) A. P. Herbert, in *What a Word!*, p. 47, remarks, 'Whenever I see a truly horrible word I look in the dictionary and find that it was used by Dr. Johnson, or was common in 1541'. He concludes from this that dictionaries 'encourage and assist the enemy' (p. 48). To his implicit argument that out-of-date uses are an irrelevance, one can but observe that, when it suits them to do so, the gripers are more than ready to insist on rare and antiquated forms of English.

Carlyle: 'There was of course long conferencing, long consulting'. To *routine* dates from 1844 and would be used by George Bernard Shaw: 'he underplays them, or routines them mechanically in the old stock manner'. To *dialogue* dates from 1595. It was used by Shakespeare in *Timon of Athens*: 'Dost Dialogue with thy shadow?' And to *message* dates from 1582, later used by Dickens in *Barnaby Rudge*: 'lettering, and messaging, and fetching and carrying'. Even to *text*, which sounds modern for obvious reasons, was first attempted in English as long ago as 1564, when the physician William Bullein wrote, 'Texte how they will texte, I will trust none of them all'.

Just as there are verbs converted from nouns about which the grumblers will grumble, so there are nouns converted from verbs that go down badly with those easily disturbed by what they find unusual. They might breeze past a defunct literary example, as when in *Paradise Lost* Milton uses *disturb* itself as a noun: 'Instant without disturb they took Allarm'. They might never stop to think of all the work on this pattern done by Shakespeare, who is credited with giving us, among others, a *scuffle* and a *gust* of wind, not to mention the *dawn*. But new instances, or what are taken to be new instances, generate much huffing and puffing—an *ask*, a *relax*, government *spend*. The commentator Robert Hartwell Fiske, particularly extreme in his views, declares that any reference to 'a *disconnect*', the noun, 'is to be reviled', and that 'All further development of this word produces only grotesqueries':* it must be satisfying to be so sure. Yet there is always the chance that what at first seems peculiar will bed in, or that what is deemed unpleasant in one context is welcome in another. When, for example, the verb to *fail* is presented as a noun in the newish expression 'epic *fail*', it is deemed by gripers to be what it names.

* *Robert Hartwell Fiske's Dictionary of Unendurable English*, 2011, pp. 131–2.

Yet in the expression 'without *fail*', *fail* as a noun is accepted in just the way the phrase describes.

Huffing and puffing about conversion is nothing new. In the course of a delightful correspondence between the struggling eighteenth-century literary couple Elizabeth and Richard Griffith, Elizabeth Griffith reports to her husband on criticism of his writing style by 'Mr. —', a first-class griper: 'that you frequently take too much Liberty with the English Language; using Words often, in a different Sense, from the common Acceptation of them; running Nouns into Verbs, and turning Verbs into Nouns again; to the Confusion of all Grammar'.*

It might appear from all this that in your attempt to undermine the edifice that is Good English, it would be an idea to follow Richard Griffith's example. Feel free—except, why limit yourself to using nouns and verbs? There are other ways to go about word-class conversion as well. For a gangster to *off* a rival may sound slangy, as a verb converted from an adverb; yet people have being 'offing' in one way or another for centuries. And after all, on the same pattern, without grammatical fuss, one can *up* the stakes and *down* tools or a drink; while to *out*, with many meanings, goes back over a thousand years. Another redoubtable verb converted from an adverb is to *atone*, derived from *at one*. As for nouns converted from adverbs, what about the *ins* and *outs*? No griper likes the verb to *diss*, shortened from *disrespect*, in effect a verb made out of a prefix.† Yet the unexceptionable verb to *bus* ('they were bussed out of the hurricane zone') is on paper even less likely, made by truncating the Latin case-ending, the dative

---

* See *A Series of Genuine Letters between Henry and Frances*, Vol. IV, p. 59, 1766. (They used pseudonyms.)
† Mr Humphrys, in *Lost for Words*, likes to *rubbish*, on the grounds that it 'has a powerful ring to it', but marks down *diss* as 'voguish', whatever 'voguish' really means.

plural -*ibus*, that forms the back end of the word *omnibus*, 'for all'. Some will object to what they interpret as an adjective used as an adverb, as in 'she sang *beautiful*' rather than *beautifully*, though this habit is widespread and entrenched.* A verb recently converted from an adjective will strike others as equally debased, as here: 'Being "favourited" is a key index within the space that signals success'.† Again, however, to *tidy* is a perfectly acceptable verb, made by the Victorians from an adjective that had until then survived unconverted for five hundred years. On adjectives, the condemned expression 'the new *normal*' converts an adjective into a noun; so too does the use of *verbals* to refer to spoken nastiness: 'Public humiliation on the streets often results in verbals, pushing and arrest' (*Guardian*). Paul C. Berg included in his 1953 *Dictionary of New Words in English* the use of *lovely* as a noun, though *lovelies* had been celebrated in English from the fifteenth century on. The derided but increasingly popular job title a 'creative' follows the same pattern. But are those who flinch at *creatives* comparably repelled by *locals*, *professionals*, *executives* and *experts*? Presumably not—though if any professional were to speak of that bugbear the 'key *deliverable*', the flinching would doubtless begin all over again.

These examples may make conversion seem like a free-for-all, but there are trends within the general practice that are considered particularly loathsome. Lewis Carroll, in 'Poeta Fit, Non Nascitur',

---

* As with 'negative concord' (see Chapter 16), dislike of this form of conversion often comes across as little more than a crudely class-marked disdain for 'uneducated' English. Yet the same habit was a foppish trait in times gone by; the only 'low' aspect to the following diary entry of 24 June 1832, written by the Cambridge academic Joseph Romilly, was its sentiment: 'An awful bad sermon from Hudleston'.

† Colin Lankshear and Michele Knobel, in *The Routledge Companion to English Studies*, Leung and Street (eds.), 2014, p. 456. (The noun form of *favourite* predates the adjective, but among those who do now 'favourite', it is the adjective that is conceived of as giving rise to the verb.)

a ditty of 1869 explaining how to write pretentious poems, advised 'That abstract qualities begin / With capitals alway: / The True, the Good, the Beautiful— / Those are the things that pay!' This advice sounds quaintly harmless today because we have abstract 'things' that pay so very much more. Take a few nouns ending with *-tion*, *-sion*, *-cion*, etc.—take, for instance, a *solution*, derived from *solve*; a *suspicion*, from *suspect*; a *decision*, from *decide*; and an *acquisition*, from *acquire*: all these abstractions are themselves regularly converted back into verbs, not least in the commercial English found in reports, pamphlets and advertisements:

> Try this, try that, keep thinking of different ways to solution the problem . . .

> When a supervisor has difficulty in getting his employees to help each other, he should suspicion several things.

> To expedite your review please begin to gather the following documents we will need to decision your loan for any of the options listed above.

> Several Reasons You Need to Acquisition Vapor Cigarette Kits.

The gripers will groan that there is no conceivable need for the hideous verb to *decision* when we already have *decide*. But quite apart from anything else, to say this is to ignore the way in which supposedly redundant words can acquire nuance. Anyone uncertain of the difference between to *proposition* and to *propose* has but to reflect on the fate of Tess in *Tess of the d'Urbervilles*.

Another trend akin to word-class conversion, and one with great potential to cause dismay among our advisers, is the use of nouns in place of adjectives,* especially several in a string, forming

---

* That is, a noun used 'attributively'. An attributive adjective comes before, and modifies, a noun: 'a *soft* heart'. An adjective that comes after a verb (usually, to *be*) is described as 'predicative': 'the light was *soft*'. Some adjectives also come

what *The Economist Style Guide* calls a 'ghastly adjectival reticule'.*
Not only will all good gripers find annoying in itself a headline
such as the BBC's 'Ski trip death girl chair-lift probe' (a headline the broadcaster, on reflection, radically altered), but they
will point out that this kind of writing can sometimes lead to
confusion. Consider the heading on a leaflet produced by the
Stagecoach bus company in 2012 to alert passengers to a change
in its rural routes: 'Bus Stops Moving'. Any passenger accidentally
reading *bus stops* as a noun and a verb, and not a noun modifying
a noun, must have been taken aback at the needless frankness of
the disclosure. In speech, a speaker's stress patterns, and on the
page, a writer's punctuation, will sometimes clarify what would
otherwise be ambiguous. With commas, the much-cited line 'nut,
screws, washers and bolts' is a list of ironmongery; without them,
screws and *bolts* become verbs, and this suddenly sounds like the
headline of a crime report—as it reputedly once was. But what
of the following headline from the *Guardian*, which partly quotes
from the article it summarises: 'Let's see some babyboomer rage
about Generation Jobless'? This either means 'Let's see some
(unspecified individual) babyboomer [noun] rage [verb] about
X', or 'Let's see some (unspecified quantity of) babyboomer rage
[noun modifying a noun] about X'. Hyphenating 'babyboomer-rage'
would tell you that it was the second, but as professional writers

---

in degrees, and are therefore described as 'gradable': 'this rug is *softer*'. A
noun, too, can be used attributively to modify a following noun, e.g. an actor
can be a *star* attraction. But it would be odd (currently) for an actor to be
described as 'seeming' *star*, or as being 'more *star*' than a rival. When a noun
convincingly crosses this line, as *fun* has, it starts to be classed as an adjective
as well. (*Starry*, unlike *star*, *is* an adjective, as, among other things, it can be
used attributively and predicatively, and is gradable.)
* A reticule is a dainty little handbag of the kind given by Jane Austen to the
intolerable Mrs Elton in *Emma*.

do not dependably care for hyphens nowadays, the lack of a hyphen cannot be taken to guarantee that it was the first.

This potential for double meaning can be put to clever use, as it is in the name chosen for the military charity Combat Stress. With *combat* as a noun modifier by one reading and a verb by another, the title tells you both the difficulty the organisation seeks to address, and what it hopes to do about it. Yet pithier is the name of the feminist organisation Object, where the title oscillates between presenting itself as a noun, the original use in English of this word, and—what it then also became—a verb.

Obviously it would be hypocritical to 'object' to *object*'s having been verbified (to use a Victorian term for this process). But of all the forms of conversion mentioned above, it is verbifying, or the magicking-up of new verbs out of existing words, that grates on the nerves of the gripers the most. *The Economist Style Guide* says 'avoid', and, 'Do not force nouns or other parts of speech to act as verbs'. Simon Heffer lands an even dirtier blow with: 'this seems to have become an especially American habit'.

Forget Swift, who, weighing up the attempts of the writer Richard Steele to make *The Spectator* more appealing to women, wrote that the results were no improvement, 'let him fair-sex it to the world's end'.* Forget Dickens, who in *Great Expectations* depicts a desperate Mr Pocket saying, 'Are infants to be nutcrackered into their tombs, and is nobody to save them?' As confirmed greats, Swift and Dickens are no doubt automatically forgiven their lexical crimes. But not so the rest of us. When Elizabeth Griffith reported to her husband the views of 'Mr. —', she mentioned a cruel further point made by this unnamed critic on the subject of Richard Griffith's habit of 'using Words often, in a different Sense, from the common Acceptation of them': 'He said

---

* See *Journal to Stella*, letter dated '*Jan.* 26, 1711–12'. On Stella herself, see also p. 92. Steele was co-founder of *The Spectator* with Joseph Addison.

that this was *trop Hazardé*, (his own Expression) and presuming, for any Writer, who had not already established a Character, sufficient to be his *own Authority*'.

Well now, let us say that you have not yet established a Character sufficient to be your *own Authority* either. Fear not! This is no barrier (far from it) to your attempting to *impact* Good English by *progressing* one or two of the horrible uses detailed in this chapter.* And if you are bold enough to go a step further, you could try to convert—or even to *conversion*†—a few words of your own. The electrified griper will endeavour relentlessly to nut-cracker your babies into their tombs. But stick with it, *routine* the process, and who knows? You may just help to make the ghastly reticules of Good English that little bit plumper.

---

* Mr Humphrys wonders when *progress* became a verb (as in, 'Network Rail will be progressing this project on the above dates'). 'Probably about the same time as "impact"', he ventures glumly. The answer to his question given by the *OED* is 1780: 'A glorious war, commenced in justice and progressed in success'. As for to *impact*, on this Mr Humphrys's guess is tantalisingly close, sort of. Again according to the *OED*, *impact* was first converted in 1781—except that that was when it became a noun, having been a verb for the previous 180 years.
† 'Which conversioning under my very nose explains my Father's rather intemperate anger': R. L. Sterup, *Bertilak of the High Desert*, 2012, p. 270.

4

BACK-FORMATIONS; IZE-MANIA

to evolute, to reliabilize

Without needing to think about it very much—possibly without thinking about it at all—we develop an understanding of multiple ways in which verbs can be created and used. But just because a new verb conforms to a governing set of rules, that does not guarantee it universal success. Indeed, many a recently coined example, unimpeachably put together, has been reviled by the gripers as ridiculous and—the old beef—redundant. This is of course excellent news for your campaign, and given your selfless resolve to rush into the front lines in the battle for our language, you may now be wondering how else, other than by conversion, horrible new verbs are generated.

One method is a process known as 'back-formation', a trick whose results are unlikely to please those noisy on the subject of Good English. But what is it exactly? The *OED* defines a back-formation as a word derived from another word in a way that might well give the impression of the derivative word's having come first. An example it provides is the verb to *burgle*. You perhaps imagine that the act of *burgling* gave rise to a name for 'one who burgles': a *burglar*. But actually it was the other way round, and the noun *burglar* preceded the verb to *burgle* by more than three hundred years. In the twenty-first century, the idea of *burgling* seems entirely acceptable, lexically; but it was received at first, in the 1870s, as a humorous coinage, defined by the *OED*, with a twinkle in its eye, as meaning to 'rob burglariously'. In a curious parallel, the noun *shoplifter* predates by over a hundred years the verb to *shoplift*, a back-formation credited to the poet Shelley.* As evidence of how disliked a back-formation can be, try Richard Grant White (who wrote of horrible words as 'monsters') on the verb to *donate*, which came hundreds of years after the noun *donation*: 'I need hardly say, that this word is utterly abominable—one that any lover of simple honest English cannot hear with patience and without offence'.

Not all back-formations are verbs. It would be natural to assume that the noun *greed* gave rise to the adjective *greedy*. Instead, *greed* is a back-formation: *greedy* came first by over 600 years. The noun *diplomat* is another example. It might be thought reasonable to suppose that its first element, the Greek *diplo*, meaning 'twofold', is intended to invoke the duplicitous or double-dealing nature of the foreign agent. Instead, *diplomat* is a nineteenth-century back-formation from the much earlier adjective *diplomatic*, itself derived from the noun *diploma*, which from the 1640s was the name for an official document notionally folded in two.† As with nouns, so too some verbs are back-formations derived from adjectives. For instance, the verb *sidle* derives from *sideling*, a medieval adjective and adverb akin to its later equivalent, *sidelong*; and the seventeenth-century verb *laze* is a back-formation derived from the earlier adjective *lazy*.

It remains that the stock idea of a back-formation is that of a verb derived from a noun. Here is a sample from the last couple

---

* *Shoplifter* looks as though it was formed by adding -*er* to the 'base' word *shoplift*. However, *shoplift* was excavated from the longer form.
† So much is it not desirable to think of a diplomat as, metaphorically, 'one who folds in two', that this feeble image puts diplomatic deviousness or 'duplicity' in a thoroughly favourable light.

of centuries given in chronological order:* 1827, to *enthuse* from *enthusiasm* (the *OED* still crossly calls *enthuse* 'ignorant'); 1861, to *diagnose* from *diagnosis*; 1864, to *sculpt* from *sculptor*; 1884, to *elocute* from *elocution*, credited in the comic form 'yellocute' to Mark Twain; 1900, to *emote* from *emotion*; 1928, to *liaise* from *liaison*, originally military slang; 1929, to *spectate* from *spectator*; 1943, to *choreograph* from *choreography*; 1960, to *surveil* from *surveillance*: 'All the time, the investigators were surveilling him surveilling them' (*Guardian*). An example not yet in the *OED*, but also in evidence for a couple of centuries, is to *conversate* from *conversation* ('Jesus used prayer to commune and conversate with God'†), while earlier examples than all of these, still dismissed as illiterate, include to *evolute*, 1735; to *opinionate*, 1599; and to *aggress*, 1570. Four of the verbs above have settled into the language and will raise the pulse of perhaps only the purest purists: to *sculpt*, *diagnose*, *choreograph* and *liaise*. But the rest may well leave the good griper in a bit of a state. To take just one, R. H. Fiske, in his heart-sinking reflections on 'unendurable' English, declares that, 'Lopped from the noun *elocution*, *elocute* is severed from its force and effectiveness', etc.

In your campaign to move Good English along, you could do worse than to push the ready-made irritants given above. As for thinking up a *new* back-formation, it perhaps strikes you that this would require more intellectual effort than you can spare. If so, happily, there is a related way to generate verbs—and ill-feeling among the defenders of Good English—that requires next to no work at all. You simply fall in with what A. P. Herbert called 'Ize-mania'.‡

---

* The dates here conform to those given by the *OED*, though most of these verbs appear to be a little older than it currently states. To *surveil* certainly is.
† Monica Downing, *Don't Blame God*, 2010, p. 21.
‡ On the question of *-ize* vs *-ise*, which in this chapter will necessarily come across as an awful muddle, see below p. 43.

The verb to *burgle* sprang up in British English at roughly the time another coinage with the same meaning, to *burglarise*, sprang up in North American usage. This second form soon filtered into British English, where it has lingered, but without ever becoming as popular as the first. Consider, however, by way of contrast, the verbs arising out of the medieval noun *jeopardy*. The back-formation to *jeopard*—yes, really—can be found in the work of Chaucer; and though Samuel Johnson, in his dictionary, confidently described to *jeopard* as obsolete, it staggered on well into the nineteenth century: in a work of 1895, George Trumbull Ladd had no qualms over writing about how to 'jeopard all sound argument in the philosophy of mind'. As *jeopard* declined, however, *jeopardise* came to the fore instead. Richard Grant White could hardly stand it. He listed *jeopardise* as not only a 'monster' but a 'foolish and intolerable word'. Ambrose Bierce, weighing up *jeopardise*, concluded similarly that—especially given the existence of *imperil*—there was 'no need for anything so farfetched and stilted'. As we now know, however, *jeopard* would fall right out of the language; *imperil* would become quaint; and *jeopardise*, after a while, would effortlessly hold sway.

Forming verbs after the pattern of *jeopardise* is nothing new. *Authorise* has been in the language since around 1400, *anathematise*, since the mid 1500s, and so on. All the same, when Ben Jonson, in his play *The New Inne*, 1631, introduced the word *problematise* into the English language, he did have a character respond to it with, 'Bless us, what's that?' And as well as this startled response, we have, in the preface to his 1594 work *Christs Teares*, the thoughts of Thomas Nashe, wit, pamphleteer and friend of Jonson, as evidence of how new verbs of this kind were received four centuries ago. Nashe, to the joy of numerous future historians of the language, wrote a lengthy riposte to his lexical 'reprehenders', including those who, he said, 'complain of my boystrous compound wordes, and ending my Italionate coyned verbes all in *ize*'. The coinages in question included to *citizenize, oblivionize, retranquilize, superficialize* and *palpabrize* (to 'feel' with a sickly hint of to 'touch up'). Nor did Nashe's reprehenders stop him going on to coin examples after 1594—*beruffianize, documentize, chamelionize, infamize,* and more—though for his writing crimes more broadly, his enemies did see to it that he was thrown into prison.

Perhaps because *-ize* or *-ise* is so easy to wield, verbs formed this way can appear lightweight and humorous. Shakespeare must have wished to raise a smile when in *Two Gentlemen of Verona* he created the idea of 'living dully sluggardiz'd at home'. Fanny Burney, when she coined 'Englishize' and 'quietize', and Disraeli, when he coined 'monologise' and 'paragraphise', were evidently both in a silly mood. And Saul Bellow cannot have been much worried by thoughts of the dictionary when in his last novel, *Ravelstein*, he had a character, marooned in a fancy car, declare, 'I sat in it, feeling imbecilized . . .'. Back in ordinary use, the verbs *philosophise, attitudinise* and *therapise* all come with the suggestion of an eyebrow half raised.

And yet plenty of verbs of this kind are not lightweight in the least, while many that may start out seeming odd are normalised fast. One that was widely hated in the past, but that rarely makes a showing in style guides today, is *finalise*: 'still objected to by many' as 'ungainly', writes Bill Bryson, just in case. But is it really? In 1982, *prioritise* was described by the *OED* as 'a word that at present sits uneasily in the language'. By 1989 the caveat had gone. And whereas a lingering Victorian entry on 'nonce' words, or one-offs, gives *pedestrianise* as an example, a later, handsome entry on *pedestrianise* itself amply demonstrates that the 'nonce' label is no longer valid. *Publicise, routinise, trivialise, legitimise* and indeed *normalise* are all early Victorian coinages. *Weaponise, incentivise* and *medicalise* are much more recent. Examples so modern that they are not yet in the *OED*, though it may not be too long before they shed their uncomfortable feel, include *otherise*, *amenitise* and *calendarise*. John Humphrys, in *Lost for Words*, declares that *anonymise*—which kicked in in the 1950s—is not a 'real verb'. What he means by 'real' he omits to explain.

A. P. Herbert thought adding -*ize* was the mark of a salesman or a 'swanker'. And he might still think so today were he to slog through a recent business report vaunting a product designed to 'commoditize hardware in the network visibility fabric market'; or a job description for an analyst who must 'develop, implement, and productionize standard and ad-hoc reports'; or a plug for an energy company that will 'work to reliabilize new fabrication processes'; or an advertisement—aimed at 'relationship managers' in 'bank operations'—promoting computer software that will enable them 'to actionize and work with customers to close the loop instantly'; or a comment in an LED patent on 'the trend of the development to smallize the electrical products'; or even the rubric of a bicycle-hire company informing potential customers that it 'does not responsibilize for any accidents, injuries or whatsoever'. Herbert might still think -*ize* was a 'salesman's' tool if he saw how *personalize* is used today, a word he called 'obscene'. Yet there are many tribes in the grip of *ize*-mania who find -*ize* (or -*ise*) handy for generating special vocabulary for their own special purposes (which is to say 'jargon'). An academic explains to fellow academics, who will understand precisely, that 'classical proofs do not readily effectivize'; a bureaucrat discusses whether to 'renewalize these industries'; a legal journal notes that 'features of governmentality are working from a distance to responsibilize state conduct'.

This deluge of examples should demonstrate how unchallenging -*ize* or -*ise* is to deploy: to generate a new verb, usually with the primitive sense of X being imposed on Y,* simply follow this despised

---

* This is not, however, the only sense given to -*ize* or -*ise*, which can also mean to 'follow a mode or a practice'. Nowadays, *womanise* (a word credited by the

method and add the suffix to an adjective or a noun. (So you know, among people who really care about this sort of thing, those who favour *-ize* consider *-ise* disagreeably French, while those who favour *-ise* consider *-ize*, though Greek, disagreeably American. You will grasp that with so much prejudice floating about, it is encouragingly hard for you to go wrong!)

In short, there is endless 'ize-izing' or 'ize-ising' or 'ise-ising' out there to *enthuse* you. And because slapping *-ize* or *-ise* on the end of a word is an easy trick, should you allow yourself to be *enticised** down this path—and once having *evoluted*† your methods and *reliabilised* the execution—you ought to find nothing much to stop you. In 1953, Paul C. Berg listed several new examples of the form that have long since fallen out of use, including *dieselise*, *redundantise* and *Coventrise*, or destroy by aerial bombardment. Like these three verbs, your concoctions may not stick. But rest assured that your slightest effort will stand as a splendid reproach to the gripers, even as they do their best to freeze the common tongue.

OED to Sir Philip Sidney) understands the *-ise* to confer this second sense, so that the verb means 'philander'. Originally, however, *womanise* was understood in the 'impose X on Y' sense, and meant something more like what we currently mean by *feminize*. As Samuel Johnson still, in the eighteenth century, explained it, to *womanise* was 'to emasculate; to effeminate; to soften'.

* '. . . the substantialist metaphysician seeks to conquer the truncated world in a self-deluded oblivion of becoming, building his artificial kingdom upon enticized and digitized effects of the endurable': Lik Kuen Tong, in *Two Roads to Wisdom?: Chinese and Analytic Philosophical Traditions*, Mou (ed.), 2001, p. 74.

† '. . . the evoluted side of the zipper is not entirely existent, for the higher Self has yet to emerge': Burton Daniels, *The Integration of Psyche and Spirit: Vol I*, 2002, p. 200.

5
THE PAST TENSE

snuck

We have looked at one or two methods for creating horrible new verbs, but another way to lay siege to Good English is by misusing verbs that already exist. And it takes hardly a minute to realise that if this is to be one's method, then the best area of attack is the past tense.

To peep through an in-depth grammar of Modern English is, for most of us, to discover what a head-spinning number of rules we faithfully observe despite having not the faintest idea that we know them. But never mind that: here we shall try to keep things simple. A regular English verb forms the past tense and the past participle with the suffix *-ed*, but irregular verbs achieve these ends in other, less regular ways. So, in regular fashion, *wink* gives *winked* and *link* gives *linked*. Less regularly, *think* gives *thought*, *drink* gives *drank* and *slink* gives *slunk*. Or consider that while *knit* gives *knitted*, *sit* gives *sat* and *split* remains unchanged. Sometimes the verbs that take *-ed* are referred to as 'weak' and irregular verbs whose vowel-sounds change as 'strong', though objectively there is nothing strong or weak about either.

It should surprise no one that with all these possibilities (and more), and given the idiosyncratic nature of English, not every verb stays in a single camp. For example, it is normal in today's British English to use both *burnt* and *burned*, both *kneeled* and *knelt*, both *quit* and *quitted*. True, *quitted* may strike the up-to-date griper as more proper than *quit*, but across eight hundred years, usage has switched back and forth between the two. Sometimes one can even use different past-tense forms of a single verb in the same sentence without straying from what the most pedantic speaker would deem correct: 'He *lit* a lamp, carried it aloft, and by its cheerful glow *lighted* his way'; or 'He *heaved* a sigh of relief as the hotel *hove* into view'. Curiosities in the development of English have also bequeathed us certain habits in how we choose between competing past participles for use as adjectives, so that we say *melted* butter but *molten* gold; a *bent* back but a *bended* knee; a *cleft* palate but a *cloven* hoof; dumb-*struck* but poverty-*stricken*.

Do we object to this muddle? No. The silliest among us may even smile on discovering that in an entry on the past tense of the verb to *creep*—its permutations spanning well over a thousand years—the Victorian compilers of the *OED* found it helpful to refer to a line from the old Scottish poem 'Will and Jean' which describes how darkness crept across a far landscape, or rather, how 'mirky shadow / Crap ower distant hill and plain'. (Modernisers of the dictionary have drawn a veil over this quotation, as they have over one about a fox who 'creepit' or 'crap' through a hole.)

Yet as with other topics, when it comes to the past tense, we find a list of special bugbears that the grumblers turn to for a spot of consensual stigmatising. One is the supposed fault of using *hung* instead of *hanged* when referring to execution: as Simon Heffer explains this, 'Pictures and pheasants are *hung*, but a man is *hanged*' (pheasants are hung when already dead). So there you have it—though ordinary English speech does not reliably mark this fine distinction, which happens to have arisen because the modern *hang* is derived from more than one antecedent verb. Another supposed area of confusion, across more than just the past tense, is one famously exemplified by a line from Byron's work *Childe Harold's Pilgrimage*. In an address to the 'deep

45

and dark blue Ocean' the poem notes that—by contrast with the 'vile strength' man successfully wields 'For earth's destruction'— out upon the 'watery plain', there is no 'shadow of man's ravage';* after all, no matter how man casts himself upon the ocean, the ocean spits him back out again: 'thou', Byron writes, addressing the deep dark waters, 'dashest him again to earth:—there let him lay'. At this, every good griper will recoil. Bill Bryson's comment on *lay* and *lie* is that 'in all their manifestations' they are 'a constant source of errors'.† Rather than cite Byron, Mr Bryson gives a quotation that begins 'Laying on his back, Dalton ...', and remarks sternly: 'Unless Dalton was producing eggs, he was lying on his back'. It is hard to see quite how Byron can have meant that the corpse of man, rejected by the ocean and washed ashore, should then produce eggs; but this certainly puts a good spin on a verse-ending that is otherwise a bit of a downer.‡

But let us not worry too much about these select nuisances; far better to go for a more general approach—because what is marvellous about forming the English past tense incorrectly is the range in the type of offence this can cause. By going wrong, you may strike the indifferent critic simply as stupid. But should you come up against fully committed gripers, you will find that you can infuriate them in three particular ways: by seeming childish, facetious or—worst of all—American.

It is mostly the province of the child to treat as regular a verb that is conventionally irregular. Among the over-sixes, *keep* usually

---

* This was before overfishing and plastic trash-vortices.
† If it sits uneasily with you that Mr Bryson puts *error* in the plural here, see Chapter 18. He himself would doubtless have conniption fits at this subheading in the *Guardian*: 'As a blues man lays to rest in the Mississippi Delta, questions linger about how he died'.
‡ A critic in the *Saturday Review*, 1 March 1879, referred to Byron's use of *lay* here as 'his Titanic error', but then fawned a little by adding '(he was Titanic even in grammar)'.

gives *kept* and *eat* gives *ate*: to say 'My tooth came out but I *keeped* it' or 'I *eated* a biscuit' is therefore likely to make you sound sickeningly babyish.* It is, however, just possible that something even worse is going on. Campaigners for the slogan 'no means no' must suffer pangs at the following squib from Alfred Crowquill's *Electric Telegraph of Fun*, a compendium from 1854 of jokes designed to amuse gentlemen on boring railway journeys. In it, a scene is painted of a young man wooing a young lady: I was, he says, 'about to imprint a kiss upon her lips, when she looked me saucily in the eyes, and with a smile upon her angelic countenance, she said, "don't!" and I *don'ted!*' Just as *do* gives *did*, *don't* conventionally gives *didn't*. But here the speaker understands *don't* to mean 'do', or in other words: act. He therefore interprets *don't* as a peculiar but regular verb, 'to *don't*', and in response to the angelic young lady, acts, and kisses her, or—as he tells it—'I *don'ted*'.

By contrast, for a writer to make a regular verb irregular in some way, or to make an already irregular verb differently irregular, speaks of play if the reader is charitable, and of airy facetiousness if not: I *knat* a woolly scarf; I *squoze* my lemon; 'Spring is sprung the grass is riz'. There may be something childish about switching your irregular forms, but using the wrong irregular past tense usually suggests that you know the standard uses and are scrambling them on purpose. The *OED*, for example, marks it as a 'Joc. variant' when James Joyce writes in *Ulysses*, 'Have a good old thunk'.†

But these two signals—infantile, playful—will be more than trumped by the dismay you are likely to cause a language purist if you can inspire the charge (frequently unjustified) that you are using an Americanism. Take *dive*. In current British English the

---

* See also Dorothy Parker's use of *fwowed* for *threw*, p. 93.
† The feel of *thunk* alters slightly when you discover that *think* and *thank* are in origin the same word.

past tense is usually weak: *dived*. In current American English it is often strong: *dove*. There is no consistency to this pattern. The British will happily say, 'I *skived* off work and *drove* into a ditch'. But try remarking that you '*dove* into the pool', and see what consternation you cause the average griper. Even worse, attempt a *snuck*. This strong past tense is increasingly successful in British English as a rival to the weak form *sneaked*. And as ever, there are those who greatly disapprove. For good measure, throw in an antiquated *gotten*, charitably preserved for us by the Americans and now on the rise again here, and you will be away.

You may be asking yourself what, really, is wrong with Americanisms. The answer you need to get hold of is that, from your perspective, there is *absolutely nothing wrong with Americanisms*. Then again, some Americans are dismayed by some Americanisms too. If ever you are accused of deploying one, you must reply with the chestnut 'I could care less'.* Or if you are feeling bullish, point out to your critic that there are terms of American origin that the British would be loath to do without—*nifty*, *bogus*, *pussyfooting*, and so on; furthermore, that there are terms of American origin without which the staunchest upholder of British values might be hard-pressed to define Britishness—to define *Englishness* itself. The *stiff upper lip* to which so many of us pretend to aspire was born in the USA. So too was the *underdog* in whose support we wrongly imagine ourselves to be distinct.

On 12 March 1711, Addison wrote in *The Spectator*, 'The Mind that lies fallow but a single Day, sprouts up in Follies that are only to be killed by a constant and assiduous Culture'. But hey, constant and assiduous Culture may not be your thing. So although with non-standard past tenses you have the choice of

---

* For more on negatives, see Chapter 15.

seeming to be facetious, childish or American, and could therefore pick the effect most likely to leave your particular audience miserable, you could just decide to mix up your regulars and irregulars scattershot. Even if you settle for this second, slapdash approach, once you have *snuck* in a despised form or two, you will be able to tell yourself that you have contributed to the unstoppable forward march of language change. Naturally, the beleaguered griper will curse you and hope that you are wrong.

6

TRANSITING TRANSITIVITY

coincide it

Another way to misuse a verb is to take one that, in the minds of a griper, is either transitive or intransitive but not both, and to use it, to that griperish mind, the wrong way round. Briefly, and without going into the complicating factors, a transitive verb has at least one direct object: 'the dog ate a poisoned rat'. An intransitive verb has no direct object: 'the dog died'. Some verbs have 'dual transitivity': 'the dog ate the rat'; 'the dog ate'. But some verbs are ordinarily used only intransitively or only transitively: we do not generally say that the dog 'died' the rat, or that a person faced with mice behind the skirting boards 'poisoned'.

Yet if 'X died Y' or 'Z poisoned' would sound distinctly peculiar to most people, there are many verbs that are in the process of crossing this divide. Simon Heffer declares that it is not legitimate to use *collapse* transitively ('one cannot *collapse* a house of cards'), even though it appears to be perfectly normal to 'collapse' this and that when required ('The search party that located the bodies, eight months after death, simply collapsed the tent over them', *Telegraph*). He also notes that, 'thanks to America', the already suspect intransitive verb to *exit*—'suspect' because he finds the Latin to be at fault—is becoming a transitive verb too. He explains that it is an 'unnecessary abomination' to have 'people exiting buildings'.

Mr Heffer is also against what he sees as exclusively transitive verbs being used intransitively, 'a price cannot *halve*', and so on. And Bill Bryson finds it necessary to warn his readers that they face the 'slight risk of censure' if they use the verb *warn* intransitively: the intransitive expression 'he warns of the risk of censure' might, once in a while, he believes, attract censure. It certainly would from Mr Heffer, who writes that '*warn* has not developed into an intransitive verb, despite an enormous effort by semi-literates over the centuries to make it do so', defending the illogic of this posture by saying that only the transitive use of *warn* is 'correct', because it is—of all things—'logical'. John Humphrys, in his second book on the English language, *Beyond Words*, 2006, reveals that he is unmoved by the 'sweet smile' of a waitress who says 'Enjoy!' to him, and wants to ask her, 'Don't you know that "enjoy" is a transitive not an intransitive verb?' A linguist would explain that in this case there is an 'unexpressed object'. The waitress herself, compelled to serve Mr Humphrys, might like to reply to his put-down that the *OED* cites intransitive uses of *enjoy* from 1380 on. Better yet, she could recite the example it gives from 1549: 'Yet he neuer enioied after, but in conclusyon pitifully wasted his painful lyfe'.*

When it comes to transitive and intransitive uses, what is perhaps oddest about the bees in the average griper's bonnet is just how few of them there are. *Exit*, *warn*, *enjoy*? The list is ridiculously small. New or new-sounding† intransitive uses, in particular, abound in current English:

> But what strikes is the utter singularity of this wild and barbarous figure. (*Guardian*)

---

* To the rejoinder 'that was 1549; this is now', see Mr Humphrys's own argument, quoted on p. 28, that we should stick with the earliest grammatical use of a word: *enjoy* was intransitive for a hundred years before it became transitive as well.

† As with *enjoy*, there may well, in this kind of example, be ancient precedents.

The idea that Wallace's curiously ugly, styleless prose style is actually a brilliant commentary on the materialistic anomie of postmodern society fails to convince, because it is so pervasive in ostensibly different voices. (*Guardian*)

Growing up in Australia, where Anzac day was a public holiday, the subject fascinated more than any other ... (*Guardian*)

Haynes assures that the scale of the job was 'utterly terrifying ...' (*Guardian*)

Any decent griper should by now be wondering desperately what strikes *whom*** (*the dispassionate observer*?), *whom* the idea fails to convince (*the average metropolitan snob*?), *whom* the subject fascinated (*Australian history buffs*?), and *whom* Haynes assures (*himself, his psychiatrist*?): in short, what the missing objects in these sentences actually are.

When a critic gives a description of a performance 'that overwhelms. It reminds one that great acting is about transformation' (*Guardian*), there is no obvious explanation for why, if it 'overwhelms', it should not also 'remind' that great acting is about something or other. The good griper is therefore likely to feel that those who form sentences on this model are ducking the effort and perhaps also the responsibility of being more specific.†

---

* (Though perhaps even a resolute griper would nowadays cast this *whom* as 'who'.)

† As a confidence trick, this is not unlike the habit among reporters who broadcast live of using an all-embracing passive to avoid plainly declaring their own ignorance. For instance, on 22 July 2013, many of them, repeatedly and with great solemnity, declared, 'It is not yet known whether the Duchess of Cambridge has given birth'. A dedicated griper will have shouted back at the wireless that only with some sort of group psychosis prevailing in the delivery room could this possibly be true; and that even then, the baby itself, in some primitive fashion, probably knew whether or not it had been born.

The lesson is a small one, but what *strikes* is that this particular form of misuse could be a subtly annoying feature of your campaign. Do, therefore, think of messing with transitivity: if you make this a habit, and then *coincide it** with other assaults on Good English, it will surely contribute towards your desired end of *overwhelming*.†

---

* 'And yet how can we speak of architecture seriously adrift and not coincide it with our contemporary moment?': Roger Connah, *How Architecture got its Hump*, 2001, p. 137; 'I mastered the early yard missions and coincided it with back jumps': Glynn Judd, *Addicted to Steel*, 2013, p. 27.
† For more on *overwhelm*, and for *underwhelm*, see pp. 129–30.

7

PHRASAL VERBS

to understand up

There is yet another way to mishandle verbs that you would do well to consider. Our smallest unmodifiable words are referred to more loosely as 'particles'. When one of these, specifically a preposition or an adverb—*off, in, out*, etc.—is placed after a verb—say, to *take*—and the two-word result has a distinct meaning, you have what for a long time has been known as a 'phrasal verb'. Nor need there be just one meaning for this unit. Using, as above, *off, in, out*, and to *take*, consider that to *take off* can mean both to 'scarper' and to 'remove'; to *take in*, both to 'shelter' and to 'delude'; to *take out*, both to 'extract' and to 'vanquish by main force'—among many other possibilities. We shall not detain ourselves here with contested classes of, fine distinctions among, or indeed other names for the phrasal verb—though you should know that we most certainly could. This is because what is of interest to us here is how their meanings are so often idiomatic.

An 'idiomatic' meaning is, as the *OED* explains, one 'not deducible from the meanings of the individual words'. Thus, in a manner non-deducible from its parts, to *send up* can mean to 'mock'; to *act out*, to 'have a tantrum'; to *crack on*, to 'continue'; to *fork out*, to 'pay'; to *screw up*, to 'get wrong'; to *rip off*, to 'swindle'. All the following meanings for to *make out* are idiomatic: to *make out* a cheque is to 'write' it; to *make out* a distant figure is to 'discern' it;

to *make out* the meaning of a code is to 'decipher' it; to *make out* that you enjoyed a wearying party is to 'pretend' you did; to *make out* on a park bench is, at the very least, to 'canoodle' there, and so on. There are, in addition, lost meanings for to *make out*. When Addison, in a *Spectator* piece of 23 July 1711, despaired at those among his readers who expected too much of his 'piece-meal' efforts, he wrote, 'it is often expected that every Sheet should be a kind of Treatise, and make out in Thought what it wants in Bulk'.

The guardians of Good English are particularly jealous of their grip on what they believe to be correct idiom. It is a sort of comfort to be in on a code, and this no doubt explains why they get shirty about the appearance of new interpretations of existing phrasal verbs, let alone about the appearance of entirely new phrasal verbs, dismissing them as slangy, and if possible (of course) as redundant. In *Lost for Words*, for example, John Humphrys roundly stigmatises 'our habit of sprinkling prepositions where they should not be', and asks, as a griper will, why the 'horrible' use 'stressed "out" as opposed to simply stressed?'

The 'redundantly' sprinkled particle that attracts most ire from the gripers is not, however, *out*—or *off* or *back* or *with*, though *The Economist Style Guide* questions the point of 'sell *off* ', 'cut *back*' and 'meet *with*', among others. It is *up*. True, an added *up* may occasionally invoke something literal. In the case of *crop up*, for instance, 'up' might be thought to convey the metaphorical force of a burgeoning wheat field, reversing the usual meaning of *crop*, which is more like 'cut down'. Yet so compelling is the use of *up* in these formations that nowadays we feel *cooped up*, not, as we used to, *cooped in*; and we metaphorically *slip up* as though weightless in an orbiting space station, though use of *slip up* predates any human experience of zero gravity: in *One Word and Another*, 1954, V. H. Collins stolidly described the example of *slip up* as 'a bad one, because one slips down'.

In the words of Bill Bryson, '*up* is often just a hitchhiker'. And where it is getting a free ride—as it is, he says, in *head up*—he rules that it should be 'unceremoniously expunged'. Naturally, this anathematising is a lost battle in many, many cases. Take to *think up*, *dream up* and *conjure up*: though it is hard to put your finger on precisely what those *up*s are up to, who—even among the gripers—is so scrupulous with *think*, *dream* and *conjure* as never to use the easy-going add-on particle?*

An example of a newly interpreted phrasal verb using *up*, found in the lexicon of computer gamers, is to *level up*, meaning to 'progress to the next stage of a game' ('he's been grinding mooks all day, trying to level up'†). Neat as this is, it will almost certainly be written off as the displeasing slang of others by those who have no need to express the idea.‡ As for *fess up*, which docks the intensifier 'con' from the front of *confess*, and puts a different intensifier at the back end instead ('fess' derived from *fateri*, Latin for 'utter'): grimly jocular, horrible and pointless, the gripers will declare. What might strike them as even worse than either, however, is the following snippet from a business dedicated to 'remote outsourcing staff', which explains—on the subject of 'search-engine optimization'—that 'It would take years before you fully understand up what SEO really is all about' (perhaps

---

* Paul C. Berg listed *think up* and *dream up* as new in 1953, when both were already roughly a century old. And *conjure up* is credited by the *OED* to Shakespeare, who, in *A Midsummer Night's Dream*, wrote the line, 'To conjure tears up in a poor maid's eyes'.

† i.e. 'He's been finding weak characters all day and continually killing them—so as to get small amounts of XP in an attempt to reach the next level.' (*XP* here means 'experience': for more on 'bovrilisation' see Chapter 21.)

‡ Though in fact *level up* in this sense is already being used outside this context, so that it would not be astonishing if in time it were to gain much wider currency as a metaphor—a substitute for *pulling your socks up*, *getting your shit together*, and so on.

it would). Equally bad must be the Mormon text, *The Book of Helaman*, 16:22, which states: 'many more things did the people imagine up in their hearts'. The belief that *up* in these uses is no more than a feeble intensifier will be justified by pointing out that *understand up* means absolutely nothing more (to the person objecting) than *understand*, and *imagine up*, absolutely nothing more than *imagine*.

However, that initial presumed redundancy guarantees neither that a new phrasal form will fade away, nor that its meaning will remain hard to define. Indeed, a phrasal verb may well in time acquire all sorts of idiomatic nuance. In an over-hasty attempt to make his point, Mr Bryson classes the *out* in *check out* and the *off* in *pay off* as examples of 'careless writing', declaring that the particles supply no special 'shade of meaning' that the verbs *check* and *pay* would lose without them. But as even a careless English speaker could tell him, *check out* is often used to imply a pleasurable act of assessment ('check out the dude in the corner'), where *check* would be comparatively dispassionate; and *pay off* tends to suggest an illicit transaction ('he paid off the witness'), where *pay*, again, can be entirely neutral ('the witness had her expenses paid'). Just as these two phrasal verbs have gained special senses over time—*pay off* meaning 'bribe' goes back to the 1940s—so, if *imagine up* has a future, there is no reliable way to predict just what it will be.

But none of this will matter to the gripers. If they see a particle as contributing no readily explainable new meaning to a verb, they will dismiss it as an iniquity—or a valueless 'tail-twister', in the words of A. P. Herbert in *What a Word!*—to be 'unceremoniously expunged'. And if it does supply a new sense to a verb, they will nevertheless condemn the new use as falling outside the dictionary. Meanwhile, let us not forget that you can also offend them by *failing* to use a phrasal form to which they have accommodated themselves: in *Right Word, Wrong Word*,

1956, V. H. Collins declares sternly: '*ring up* (on the telephone) is not only permissible but compulsory, *ring* here without *up* being incorrect'. This stricture sounds risible now, and can only have been prompted then by numerous people failing to abide by it.

Phrasal verbs, as we have already noted, lend themselves to slang uses, or at the very least to informality, as in the examples *dish out* for 'allot', *bugger off* for 'disappear' (perhaps irresponsibly), *duff up* for 'assault', *conk out* for 'expire', *knock up* for 'make pregnant', and so on. Some of them also come across as childish, as when to *tell on* is used to mean 'betray': 'I'm going to tell on you'. Dickens was certainly going for a colloquial touch in *Pickwick Papers* in 1837 when he had a character ask, '"I say, old boy, where do you hang out?"' And when W. S. Gilbert used the same expression in a volume of his *Bab Ballads* from 1869, it was intended to add a comic note: 'For thirty years this curious pair / Hung out in Canonbury Square'. But not only is it *not* axiomatic that a phrasal verb will seem slangy—to *take on* a challenge is perfectly formal, as is, linguistically, to *hand over* a ransom—it is not axiomatic either that it will seem less informal as it becomes more established, as one might vaguely suppose. To *leave off*, meaning to 'stop', is currently at the informal end of language use. Yet Addison, remembering with scorn those women who would receive visitors in the morning while still in bed, and undressed, wrote impeccably in *The Spectator*, 21 April 1711: 'As the Coquets, who introduced this Custom, grew old, they left it off by Degrees'.

And, oddly perhaps, we can find ourselves missing those particles if they happen to get dropped again. When Dickens used *hang out*, it meant to live in a place. By the time W. S. Gilbert used it, it could also mean, as now, to idle somewhere. Many people find the idea of merely 'hanging', as it is often expressed these days—that is, *hanging out* without the *out*—yet more slangy than the phrasal form it replaces.* Meanwhile, millions who might once have said, 'That's that *sorted out*', now say simply, 'That's that *sorted*': to one such as Simon Heffer, the pithily reduced *sort* is a 'modern abomination'. The bare form *pass*, meaning 'die', may also sound awkward, or perhaps American, to those more used to using, or to hearing—if both forms of the expression are beneath them—to *pass away* or *pass on*. Chaucer's Squire, however, cannot have sounded American to anyone (for obvious reasons) when he said, 'Myn harm I wol confessen er I pace'.

Removing the particle from a phrasal verb is not the only way to duff it up a little. In the example to *knock out*, it is *knock* and not *out* that takes the verb endings: 'The boxer *knocked* out his opponent'. But when this phrasal verb is abbreviated, becoming *KO*, it is treated as a compound, meaning that the verb endings move to the end of the whole unit: 'The boxer *KO'ed* his opponent'. Presumably no one would be much worried by the form of either sentence. But what about this description of scientists 'who succeeded in extending by factor 5.5 the life span of nematode *Caenorhabditis elegans* if two genes were knock-outed'?[†] In their unmediated (and even their mediated) reflections, freely broadcast to the world, some people seem to be that bit hastier than others to turn phrasal verbs into compound verbs: 'I saw one of the live performances and she even knock-offed the choreography'; 'The owner of the vehicle tip-offed the police and there was a chase'; 'Jesus Christ himself was brought to trial using trump upped charges'.

John Steinbeck, in his *Journal of a Novel*, the entry for 13 February 1951, wrote: 'one thing we have lost—the courage to make new words or combinations. Somewhere that old bravado has

---

* To *hang*, in this sense, has actually been in use since the 1940s.
† Vladimir Skulachev, in *Formal Descriptions of Developing Systems*, Nation, Trofimova, Rand and Sulis (eds.), 2003, p. 76.

slipped off into a gangrened scholarship'. On the evidence of English phrasal verbs, how wrong he was! The recent examples to *fess up*, *big up* and *sex up* all now appear in the *OED*. To *flag up*, *grass up* and *bin off* * have yet to make a showing. This patchy record is only to be expected. Popular phrasal verbs in English are so changeable, as the days, months and years go by, that an earnest dictionary and its lexicographers can hardly hope to keep up. Some time in the future, it is quite possible that they will hardly be able to *hope up* that they can keep up either. Once you have fully *understood up* how useful this chronic instability is for your campaign—whatever *understanding up* comes to mean—there should be nothing much to stop you. Go ahead, seize on some particles and sprinkle them about at will—but do also prepare yourself for the scorn the gripers will mete out in reply.

---

* '. . . this floozy had binned him off in the type of manner that she's now been binned off herself in turn': Mark England, *Insularfield*, 2014, p. 232; 'They've binned off that rather wild-looking man from the agency': Janet Davey, *By Battersea Bridge*, 2013, p. 231.

8

COMPOUNDS IN GENERAL

to rage-quit

You may have noticed a few chapters ago that Thomas Nashe's sixteenth-century reprehenders complained not only about verbs he had formed with *-ize*, but also about his 'boystrous compound wordes'. In the 1590s, Nashe gave the language its first known uses of *owl-light*, meaning 'dusk'; of *potluck*, as we still use it; of *gravedigger*, ditto; of *chatmate*, meaning exactly what it sounds as though it means; and also (to the delight of anyone who ever stumbles across it) of *windfucker*, as a variant term for a kestrel. He is credited with the adjectives *homespun* and *frostbitten*; with the verb to *brickwall*, not unlike the modern verb to *stonewall*; and with the idea of an *afterlife*—though by this, disturbingly, he meant 'old age'. These are all examples of compounds, in which, in the most general terms, two or more words that stand happily alone have been spliced.* Nashe used analogy to defend his 'boisterousness' in creating his compound forms, noting that apothecaries were wont to give curatives made of mixed ingredients, and promising that a person had only to 'graft wordes as men do their trees, to make them more fruitfull'.

The term *chatmate* may sound modern for 1599; but what about *stopgap*, which is half a century older, or *busybody* from William

* A word that stands happily alone is described by linguists as a 'free element'. (It contrasts with a 'bound element', e.g. *-ing*, which does not.)

Tyndale's 1526 version of the New Testament?* Actually, these words are all recent set beside our earliest compounds. It is lovely to imagine *harebells* in 1387, touching that *sweetheart* can be found in 1290, terrific that we have had *Christmas* since 1123. However, compounding in English goes back much, much further still. The words *earð* or 'earth', and *land*, in evidence from around 725, were put together in the dawn of recorded English to give *yrðland* or 'earth-land', meaning arable land. Comparably remote, the *hydgild* was a fine paid in place of being flogged: the first part meant 'hide' or skin, while a *gild* or 'yield' was a payment made in recompense, a sense of *yield* that can be dated back to 604. Other venerable compounds from among countless examples include *regnwyrm* or 'rain-worm', our earthworm, so called then because worms like to come up out of the ground when it is drizzly; *biabread* or 'bee-bread', a honeycomb with the honey still in it; *musfealle* or 'mouse-fall', a mousetrap; and the *gangpyt* or 'go-hole', otherwise a privy: we preserve *gang* for the broad meaning of 'go' in such words as *gangplank* and *gangway*. And if 'bee-bread', 'hide-yield' and 'mouse-fall' are no longer used in English, *headache* certainly is, which dates from around the year 1000.†

As Nashe implied, a compound word has the potential to be more than the obvious sum of its parts. Among those examples listed above that come from his writing, the noun *chatmate* may be literal, but the verb to *brickwall* is metaphorical, and a kestrel imagined as a *windfucker* glides with lyrical ambiguity between the two. Speakers of the earliest known version of what we call English fashioned numerous of these poetic compounds so as to multiply the meanings that could be wrung from the individual

---

* Tyndale was executed for daring to put the Bible into English.
† Use of the word *headache* to mean, metaphorically, a problem, is only a hundred years old, and provoked much indignation among commentators in the middle of the last century.

elements of their language. The term 'kenning',* taken from medieval Icelandic, is used for the roundabout or metaphorical ornaments found in Old Norse writing, and kennings were much used in Old English too. Thus *banhus* or 'bone-house' invoked the body, and *merehengest* or 'sea-steed', a ship. In another antique example, *modhord*, the first part, *mod*, is the etymological forebear of the modern word *mood*, and shares Indo-European roots with *mode*. In early Old English, however, it had meanings akin to inner spirit, soul, thought, heart, desire, and more. *Hord*, meanwhile, 'store' or 'treasure', gives us the present-day *hoard*. The word *modhord* or 'mood-hoard' could therefore be thought of as meaning something like 'treasure trove of thought and soul'. But in practice it is usually translated with the word *mind*, which is snappier, but perhaps no more illuminating.

The poetic nature of compounds leaves obvious potential for changes in their sense. The *merehengest* or 'sea-steed', we have seen, was a ship. Its equivalent, *seahorse*, was first used in English as a name, not for the little upright fish, but for a walrus. The earliest meaning of *deapbed* or 'death-bed' was a grave. When Shakespeare coined *bedroom*, he meant space in a bed. And for four and a half centuries, *wormhole*, also credited to Shakespeare, meant a hole made by a worm: only in 1957 was *wormhole* adopted to describe hypothetical channels in space and time. In the nineteenth century, to *die hard* was criminal slang meaning—according to the 1823 edition of Francis Grose's *Classical Dictionary of the Vulgar Tongue*—to 'shew no signs of fear or contrition at the gallows; not to whiddle† or squeak'; felons were urged to take death without a murmur 'for the honour of the gang'. But when *diehard* entered military slang as a noun, *hard* was taken to imply the exact opposite of this impressive restraint, so that a *diehard*

---

* The verb to *ken*, meaning 'make known', dates in English from 975.
† To *whiddle* or 'peach' was to inform on your fellow criminals.

has come to be understood as one who, against overwhelming odds, puts up maximum resistance. In *The Old Curiosity Shop*, Dickens confidently upturned the normal sense of *old-fashioned*, and used it instead to describe a 'small slipshod girl' who seemed to have been created ancient from the word go.

Previous chapters in this book are dotted with examples of compounds that are hundreds of years old: *hogwash*, *pitfall*, *bugbear*, and so on. But new compounds are also constantly being formed in English. Sometimes this is because a novel entity needs naming—*shell shock* and *clickbait*, a *bar-code* and a *tape deck*, to *kick-start*, *spacewalk* and *photobomb*. Sometimes, however, a new compound merely gives edge to an existing idea—*badass*, *dickweed*, *shitstorm*, *groupthink*, *cold-call*, *scope-creep*. And then there are new compounds whose appeal lies, for the most part, in their being pithy, nailing what it previously took a whole phrase to express—the verb *rage-quit*: to abandon a task in a state of foot-stamping frustration;* *buzzkill*: to quench a general mood of excitement;† *hot-desk*: to maximise the value of a single workspace by splitting its use between several workers across more hours than one alone would be able or willing to labour; *friend-zone*: to keep at arm's length a suitor who is charming, delightful, and so on—but no more than that, whom one would like to retain, if humanly possible, as a pal.

It perhaps hardly needs saying at this point that the business of sticking two words together to make a third is among the easier ways to come up with a repulsive novelty. And if you struggle to make an impression this way, you can at least take comfort

---

* *Rage-quitting* comes into the language courtesy of computer gamers, e.g. '. . . people work so hard on their avatars and would rage-quit if permadeath was introduced': Eric Feka, *I was an Internet Addict*, 2012, p. 101.

† The noun-plus-verb form exemplified by *buzzkill* may, to some, sound stupid and 'made up', but older compounds on this pattern present no such difficulty: *hoodwink*, *browbeat*, *breastfeed*.

from the failed efforts of acknowledged geniuses. Read Shake-speare, and you will meet many such inventions that died a death—the nouns *clotpole* and *counter-caster*; the adjectives *high-lone* and *nookshotten*, 'of irregular, angled form' according to the *OED*; the verbs to *weather-fend* and *land-damn*—which not even the *OED* can explain. Sir Philip Sidney coined *fear-babes* and *navel-string*. Milton gave *homefelt* a whirl. Gerard Manley Hop-kins tried *spendsavour*; James Joyce, *smilesmirk*; and on and on. At the same time, many literary efforts have stuck. Shakespeare is also credited with giving us *lacklustre*, *eyeball*, *dewdrop* and *fairyland*; Sidney, with inventing the *deathblow*. Milton appears to have coined *awestruck*; Dryden, *day-dream*; Coleridge, *soulmate*.

If you feel timid about putting words together like this but still have a yen to use compounds in your campaign, verbifying existing compounds is a good alternative manoeuvre—bound to set the gripers shuddering. As ever, there are plenty of estab-lished examples of this move that nobody now notices or dislikes. What of the sixteenth-century *buttonhole* becoming the nineteenth-century 'to *buttonhole*'; the seventeenth-century *ring-fence* becoming the eighteenth-century 'to *ringfence*'; the eighteenth-century *side-step* becoming the twentieth-century 'to *side-step*'; or the seventeenth-century *pinpoint* becoming the twentieth-century 'to *pinpoint*'? All of these oddities, as they must once have seemed, are now established within Good English, but no agreeable precedent along these lines will stop the wretched griper fuming at new examples: among our lexical *fearbabes*, un-familiarity breeds contempt. The author of each of the quotations below will have caused anguish to many a naysayer. By learning from their efforts, you could too:

> Business leaders in Davos keen to mainstream circular economy. (*Guardian*)

City should 'watchdog' its own problems.   (*Baltimore Sun*)

Walker Said To Handshake On Statewide Voucher Plan. (*WPR News*)

Don't broad-brush the semiconductor market. (*EDN Network*)

FSA calls on IFAs to 'sense-check' risk profiling approach. (*Moneymarketing*)

My career as a chef has been springboarded by at least five years.   (*Chicago Tribune*)

The prospective purchaser chooses not to stakehold the deposits ...   (Estate Agents Authority, Hong Kong)

9
PARTICULAR COMPOUNDS

to downstream

The compounds at issue in this chapter differ from those of the last only inasmuch as each here includes one of the little indeclinable words or 'particles' that we met in Chapter 7: *in*, *out*, *up*, *down*, *off*, *on*, *over*, *under*, etc. We will therefore particularise these compounds as 'particular' compounds, remembering that this is not a designation known to anyone outside these pages. The reason for making this subcategory is that new examples of these particular compounds are a wonderful source of annoyance to the gripers. For our purposes, they deserve to be looked at on their own.

Consider the verbs to *outsource*, *upsell*, *offshore*, *inbox*, *outreach*, *upstream*, *offline* and *input*: is a single one of these embraced by the guardians of Good English? Even *upload* would probably strike their sensitive ears as a lumpy modern contrivance. And many reviled nouns are fashioned in the same manner. What griper likes an *opt-in*, a *rollout*, *throughput*, or, perhaps even worse, a *workaround*—as when a Department of Health document explains that it 'provides suggestions of best practice and workarounds used by NHS organisations to produce reference costs from PLICS data'? This type of compound gives us adjectives too, so that we can have *ongoing* problems, *upscale* suburbs, an actor's *breakout* role, the *offline* world. Football has coined its own example in the *wantaway* player—one who would like to shift team. As the *Telegraph* notes, 'Brighton are again likely to make do without wantaway midfielder Liam Bridcutt'; and it is perhaps only a matter of time before *wantaway* is applied more broadly—to errant spouses, say, or MPs flirting with rival political parties. Kingsley Amis described *ongoing* (a word in play for at least 150 years by the time he passed judgement) as a 'popular horror' and explained that 'nobody who uses it in ordinary conversation without some sort of jeer or sneer is to be trusted'. But should we also, therefore, just to be on the safe side, jeer and sneer at the fool who is sunny and *outgoing*? Not for the first time, it appears that the pool of hate-words obsessing our advisers is much smaller than it needs to be. *The Economist Style Guide* dutifully picks out two examples, and declares that *upcoming* is 'better put' as *forthcoming* (merely more antique); *ongoing*—one of its 'horrible' words—as *continuing*.

One wonders quite how Amis would have felt about the verbs to *outbring*, *ingo* and *upcheer*. First use of *outbring* is credited by the *OED* to King Alfred—King Alfred who actually named our language 'English'. *Ingo* is credited to the Venerable Bede. And it was the Countess of Pembroke, sister of Sir Philip Sidney, who in the 1590s coined *upcheer* for one of her ravishing translations of the Psalms: 'But my oreloaden soule thy selfe upcheare'. There are innumerable other words on this pattern lost in the back catalogue of our language. Is it not beguiling to know that, far away in the year 1000, the *upspring* of the day referred to the rising of the sun; of the night, to the rising of the stars?

The interest of literary figures in these particular compounds by no means ended with the Countess of Pembroke. In his 1819 poem *Mazeppa*, Byron wished to invoke the extremity of the excess punishment suffered by his titular hero, bound naked to a galloping horse. Faced with a three-syllable gap at the start of the line in question, what he invented for the job was *overtortured*: 'he who dies', says Mazeppa, 'Can die no more than then

I died. / O'ertortured by that ghastly ride'.* George Eliot seems to have been especially open to this type of splicing. She was quick to employ the then-new noun *outlash*; she revived the moribund *outleap*; she made *outfling* metaphorical. She converted *instreaming* from an adjective to a noun, and the medieval verb *outshut* into an adjective: 'the moan of outshut winds'. Lewis Carroll, too, was inspired by such words when creating his celebrated lexicon of nonsense: 'All mimsy were the borogoves; / And the mome raths outgrabe'.†

With this sort of history behind the subset of compounds we are now contemplating, it might be thought that critics would exercise caution when deriding new examples. After all, though a griper must wince at being told by the Scottish Government that 'cross-sectional surveys' should be able 'to output income data'—not least because the griper finds the verb *output* preposterous‡—how is it worse than an example we are more used to, e.g. another word ascribed to King Alfred: *understand*? As it happens, *output*, meaning 'exclude' or 'expel', has been in the language since the 1380s, and has been used in the sense the Scottish Government gives it above for over a hundred and fifty years. As for *understand*: a quibbling Viola in Shakespeare's *Twelfth Night* makes a joke out of a word no purist would stop to question, alerting us to the funniness of its parts when she says,

---

* *Overtorture* finds an echo in the twentieth-century coinage *overkill*, whose original, non-figurative meaning, as defined by the *OED*, was 'Military destruction in excess of strategic requirements'.
† It is clear from a remark made by Humpty Dumpty in *Through the Looking-glass* that Carroll intended *outgrabe* to be an irregular past-tense form: '"outgribing" is something between bellowing and whistling'. But later writers have ignored this, e.g. Alan Dean Foster in *Montezuma Strip*, 1995, and in *Trouble Magnet*, 2006: 'the police used less powerful versions of the same device to subdue juice addicts who outgrabed'; 'His tone grew intense, the way it did when he was outgrabed'.
‡ 'Preposterous': putting before what should come after.

'My legs do better understand me, sir, than I understand what you mean'.

Bede's *ingo*, dating from around 900, meant to go in, or 'enter'. And that was it. But as we know, the particles we are discussing here can be interpreted in many ways, and it follows that the compounds that use them can be too. What might the verbs *onlight*, *onopen* and *outbeard* have meant? Graspably—though one would be unlikely to guess it—*onlight*, in the twelfth century, had the meaning 'alleviate'; *onopen*, in the thirteenth century, meant 'make intelligible'; and *outbeard*, a sixteenth-century coinage, meant 'outdo through a show of defiance'. If these definitions do not come readily to mind when we look at the words now, then it should be no surprise to discover that compounds of this type are liable to change sense over time. We have already seen this with to *output*, for which the current meaning is relatively recent: what the Authorized Version of the Bible calls a soul that 'shall be cut off from among his people', an earlier version of the same line, from a Bible of the 1380s, gives as a soul that 'shal be out putte from his peplis' (Num. ix. 13). The verb *overwork*, in Old English, did not suggest driving to excess labour, but instead the act of decorating a surface. The noun *outcome* long ago meant the time of year when days lengthened and winter passed. And the adjective *inbred* was for many centuries free of all suggestion of a limited gene pool. When in 1592 Henry Smith, a miserable clergyman-poet, wittily exclaimed, 'O sin-bred hurt! O inbred hell!', he was referring to crimes committed entirely by himself.

Of course, these multiple meanings do not always neatly succeed one another. A compound of this type that has had many overlapping meanings is *income*. *Income* is far from being the twin of *ingo*. It is true that *incuman* started in Old English as a verb meaning to 'come in'. It subsequently also became a noun meaning an 'entrance', or in other words, a 'coming in'. The *OED* cites a 1566 translation of Horace that still used it in this sense: 'At mine income, I lowted lowe, and muttred full demure'. In the seventeenth century, however, use of this word was greatly expanded, so that it suddenly became possible to describe how the faithful might dare to hope for *incomes* of God into their souls. Less desirably, an *oncome*, from 1175, also then later called an *income*, referred to a physical tumour, morbid swelling or unpleasant visitation. By the early sixteenth century, Tyndale could write in his translation of the New Testament of 'incommers beynge falce brethren, which cam in amonge wother' (Gal. ii. 4): there is a strand of British sensibility today that continues to use *incomers* in much this fashion (indeed, its use is currently on the rise). And immigrants in the Tudor period were also referred to simply as *incomes*.* By the mid 1500s, *income* had further begun to be used to mean an entry fee. Then at last, in a document of 1601—so the *OED* has it—we find the first use of *income* in the sense most commonly given to it now: revenue and earnings. An entrance, divine illumination, boils, immigrants and revenue: *income* demonstrates the huge latitude in the potential meanings of compounds formed on this pattern.

It should by now be apparent that these compounds are fundamental to English as we know it. (Would England even *be* England without the odd *downpour*?)† Words of this type are being generated all the time—leaving the huffers and puffers alienated by the cultural *crossover*, the arty *mashup*; enraged by businesses *offshoring* and *inboxing*; outraged by any such assemblage as the one in which Swansea University declares that grant-holders (in an echo of the Scottish Government's wanting 'to output income data') 'can input outcomes information'. In

---

* In early Old English, and up until around 1600, strangers and foreigners could also be referred to as 'outcomes'.
† You might think not, and yet we have had 'downpours' for no more than a couple of hundred years.

your assault on Good English, you could, as ever, settle for adopting the odd horrible example of such a word as it happens to come your way. But you could also *upman** and attempt to interpret an old one anew. Better yet, you could endeavour to *output* and *downstream* your own novelties on this pattern. If you feel brave enough to try, you will find the language more than ready to accommodate your efforts; the gripers, anything but.

---

* 'First of all continue action and allow, even encourage, the upmanning': Charles Woolfson, John Foster and Matthias Beck, *Paying for the Piper: Capital and Labour in Britain's Offshore Oil Industry*, 1996, p. 197.

IO

PORTMANTEAU WORDS;
MERGING; METANALYSIS

webinar, alright, nother

Given a campaign to aim a few kicks at the putative boundaries around Good English without expending too much effort in the process, a person might justly ask: why bother uniting two words whole and entire, when one can instead simply mush a few together—and so what if a bit of lexical matter gets lost in the process?* Put another way, when in 1855 Lewis Carroll wrote a line destined to become famous in 'Jabberwocky', 'All mimsy were the borogoves', what did he mean by *mimsy*?

Humpty Dumpty, in *Through the Looking-glass*, helpfully answered this very question, saying that *mimsy* 'is "flimsy" and "miserable"'. Carroll used much suggestive mixing of this kind in his nonsense writing: *slythy* (in the phrase 'slythy toves', later re-spelt *slithy*) mixed *lithe* with *slimy*; and *chortle*, which he also invented, combined *chuckle* and *snort*. Modern dictionaries call this type of coinage a 'blend', for obvious reasons. A century ago they were sometimes referred to as 'contaminations'. Humpty Dumpty compared the results to a portmanteau, or double-sided

---

* That is to say, so what if parts of the 'base' words might be lost. (NB Paul C. Berg found it necessary in 1953 to explain to his readers that 'so what?' meant 'what of it?')

suitcase, because they give 'two meanings packed up into one word'; and for us 'portmanteau words' will do.

We use them all the time, but some go down quite badly. *The Economist Style Guide*, for example, classes *guesstimate* as one of its 'horrible' words without stopping to wonder why it was ever wanted. (It happens that as the accuracy implied by the verb to *estimate* declined in the second half of the eighteenth century, the phrase *precise estimate* became increasingly popular, and it must have been through a perceived need to stop this rot that in the early part of the twentieth century, the *guesstimate* slipped into the language.) A slightly older portmanteau word regularly cited to exemplify the form is *smog*, a blend of *smoke* and *fog* inspired by the dreadful air pollution of the late Victorian period. Going back a century further still, we find the *OED* accepting that it is 'plausibly conjectured' that *flabbergast* blends *flabby* and *aghast*. Nor was Lewis Carroll the first notable writer to try his hand at creating portmanteau words. In a letter of 1780, Fanny Burney described how, in response to an impertinent speech, she 'began to feel monstrous glumpy', mixing *glum* and *grumpy*— *grumpy* being a word she herself had previously launched in her novel *Evelina*. And sure enough, Shakespeare, too, had his own moment of fun along these lines, causing Fluellen, his Welshman in *Henry V*, to say, 'His face is all bubukles', a word that appears to blend *bubo*, meaning 'abscess', and *carbuncle*, meaning 'boil'.

A wished-for portmanteau word does not always suggest itself so easily. When the combination of ever-growing ecological concerns and a recession made a virtuous necessity of holidaying at home, the word *staycation* seemed almost to offer itself up, and stuck. By contrast, although the bumblesome act of texting while walking—so often a means of making other pedestrians glumpy—would seem an even better spur for some sort of blended verb, attempts to push *walkxting* and *pedexting* have utterly failed; and what else fits the bill?

Naturally, in addition to *glumpy* and *bubukle* and *pedexting*, there have been many failed portmanteau words along the way. When the *Daily Express* coined *sexsational* in 1928, it must have had high hopes for the term as a laster; but though *sexsational* muddles on, it has never become mainstream. George Orwell and C. S. Lewis both used the cleverly overlapping *scientifiction* for what we now call *sci-fi*—their version perhaps doomed by awkward questions about how, when spoken, it should be stressed. The *cinemaddict*, listed among Paul C. Berg's new words in 1953, never made it into the *OED*. And as for *conglomewrite*—used repeatedly by the poet Paul Muldoon to cover a subtle, marginless effect of gathered allusion—well, he can hardly have cherished great hopes of this becoming a standard term.*

Nevertheless, creating portmanteau words for in-between or liminal entities, such as smog and guesstimates, does make poetic sense. The modern term *kidult* reflects this impulse; so too does *anticipointment*: 'The anticipointment of the prequel trilogy may have trashed the franchise'.† A feeling bitterer by far lay behind the name given in 1819 to the killing by cavalrymen of work-less, starving and unrepresented people of the north at St Peter's Field, Manchester: in a satirical gesture to the recent Battle of Waterloo, a sympathetic newspaper popularised the title by which this event has been known ever since: the 'Peterloo Massacre'.

A grey area is not always a good place to be. And if the term *infomercial* feels deceitful because it fails to draw a clear line

---

* See *To Ireland, I*, 2000, pp. 60, 110 and 131, and *The End of the Poem: Oxford Lectures in Poetry*, 2006, p. 27.
† So too, indeed, does *cankle*. The ankle is no longer celebrated in quite the way it once was (*Blackwood's Edinburgh Magazine*, September 1862, warned its readers against lavishing 'incautious admiration upon the set of a well-turned ankle'). Yet now, when a woman's ankle is deemed to be insufficiently distinct from the calf above, those who feel superior about this sort of thing murmur *cankle* with a coldly confident sneer.

between its parts, the *cosmeceutical* is worse. In using this word, the makers of beauty creams and other such products hope to convey the sense that their wares will have a lasting, measurable effect; yet by not calling their products medicines, they avoid the laws that would compel them to prove that their creams actually work.

Despite the distastefully shifty uses above, many portmanteau words sound childish, or convey a feeling of silliness. Dickens, in *Bleak House*, was undoubtedly poking fun at wordy, expensive, 'ceremonious' legal fuss when he came up with *wiglomeration* as a mix of *periwig* and *conglomeration*. And a term like *sheeple*, referring to biddable herds of humans, uses its comic feel to reinforce the contempt implicit in its meaning: 'next year you're all going to remove your credit cards from your wallets like the pathetic unthinking sheeple you are and purchase about 749m copies' (*Guardian*). The adjective *glocal*—*global* blended with *local*—for all the ethical thinking behind its use, will be undone in the minds of many because, simply, it sounds daft; *webinars*, 'Web seminars', will sound no better to those unused to them; and the injunction *chillax* tends to come inflected with irony for the same reason. Who would have imagined that *ginormous*, combining *gigantic* and *enormous*, originated as forces slang in the Second World War? Decades later, it still sounds babyish.

Some words get blended with others so regularly that the shortened part comes to qualify as what is called a 'combining form'. There are classical prototypes for this manoeuvre. *Electro-*, for example, now forms a 'bound element', used in *electroplate*, *electrostatic* and *electromagnetic*—and in *electrocute*, coined in 1889 out of *electro-* and *execute*. Ambrose Bierce said hotly of *electrocution*, 'To one having even an elementary knowledge of Latin grammar this word is no less than disgusting, and the thing meant by it is felt to be altogether too good for the word's inventor'. Still, it is more usually words generated using English combining forms that inspire this kind of disdain. Some examples seem resolutely unserious: imagine a person, in a state of rapture after eating too much chocolate, claiming to have had a *chocgasm* after a *choctastic chocathon*: not only *choc-*, but *-gasm*, *-tastic* and *-athon* all now function as vaguely silly combining forms. Similarly, though the Watergate crisis brought down an American president, adding *-gate* to a word associated with a scandal—as in 'Plebgate'—now serves to trivialise an act that may be deeply immoral. Simon Heffer gives the following exasperated instruction to his readers, that if they spot a new word on this pattern, 'regard the joke as already over, and move on'. Even Oliver Kamm, author of a style guide that informs its readers that they 'can' write in all sorts of griper-defying ways, says foot-stampingly of *-gate* that it 'doesn't mean anything'.*

Reflect for a moment on the idea of a *ginormous fantabulastic webinarathon*,† and you will see how an excess of portmanteau words and jolly combining forms is calculated to make the poor griper feel ill. However, if that thought inspires you to try to dream up your own new examples, do be careful to avoid taking the sting out of them with beguiling wit. Parents may despair at the state of their teenage children's bedrooms, but who can resist a smile on first hearing the word *floordrobe*? And would there even be such a thing as 'literature' if no writer had ever practised *beditation*?

While we are on the subject of mashing words together, let us pause briefly to consider two objects of special hatred in our language, the supposed non-words *alright* and *nother*. The unitary

---

* See *Accidence Will Happen: The non-pedantic guide to English Usage*, 2015, pp. 191–2. (One suspects Mr Kamm's readers are more likely to be concerned about whether they *may*. On his approach to verbal propriety see also pp. 79 and 133.) It is a curious aspect of the Plebgate affair that it really did hinge on the use of a gate.

† As in: 'Just Imagine . . . a shift from *I* Illness to *WE* llness . . . World Day of Interconnectedness . . . a webinarathon . . . much needed for the 21st Century'.

alright, a merged form of *all right*, has for generations been written off as dismally illiterate. (As a side point, *alright* as *ealrihte*, meaning 'exactly', predates *all right* by several hundred years, while *dismal*—a word no one questions—is a merged form of *dies mali*, 'evil days'.) In a typical example of scorn, drawn from the work of Wilfred Whitten and Frank Whitaker, *Good and Bad English: A Guide to Speaking and Writing*, 1939, we find the exhortation: 'Never—*never*—write "alright." It is all wrong (not alwrong)'. They declare without explaining it that 'the two ideas co-operate better than they unite'. And custom has not staled this line of thought. Bill Bryson explains that *alright* 'ought never to appear in serious writing'. Kingsley Amis calls it a 'one-word travesty'. Mr Heffer tells us we should avoid it 'fervently'. In short, to those who flinch at it, *alright* looks as lazily shoved together as *a lot* does when it appears in the *Telegraph* as *alot*: 'Fairly or unfairly, there is alot of pressure on Caicedo's shoulders'. Yet almost everyone concedes that, given *although*, *albeit*, *already*, *always*, and so on, the compulsion to damn *alright* is irrational: as the *OED* puts it, there is 'no cogent reason' for making it two words, and a great deal of history to justify its being one.* What we now unworriedly give as *Hallowe'en* was long ago called, in a spectacularly crumpled manner, *Alhallowevin*. And not only did *alone* start out as *all one*, but it then, by a process known as 'aphesis',† lost the unstressed initial vowel to give us *lone*—upon which Shakespeare is credited with having formed the adjective *lonely*. (If only we had had no

---

* In *Right Word, Wrong Word*, 1956, V. H. Collins cites the ambiguous sentence 'Your answers are all right' to show how a sanctioned contrast with *alright* might occasionally be helpful.

† By aphesis, *acute* has given us *cute*; *esquire*, *squire*; *awayward*, *wayward*; and so on. (The term 'apocope' is used to describe losing a letter or syllable from the back of a word, e.g. *withal* having its *all* clipped, or *ago* being shaved down from *agone*.)

need of *this* one-word travesty.)* Furthermore, what about *as*? To quote the *OED* once again, this dear little word was created by the 'progressive phonetic reduction' of the Old English *ealswa*—a word that has survived separately as *also*, formed from the parts *all* and *so*. (Where are the purists now?) And it is not all *all*-words either. For instance, until the sixteenth century, there was no *partaking*; there was instead *part taking*.

You might think that with this abundance in the language of higgledy-piggledy lexical fusing, the gripers would be grateful that the form *alright* is so simple and clear. But that would be to misunderstand the nature of the fight. The more arbitrary their dislike of a given word, the more honour they are likely to invest in insisting that it is incorrect, and possibly not a word at all. You may feel, as a novice in the battle to misuse English on purpose, that you have enough to do already; that *alright* is everywhere; and that it has no need of your help. But it is not everywhere. The gripers still fight to keep it away from what they call 'serious' writing; and even Mr Kamm, who rules on *alright* that 'it's fine to go ahead and use it', is too refined to do so himself. When, for example, he writes on pedants and the English language, his conclusion is that 'they seem curiously disinterested (all right, *uninterested*) in it'. Fired up by this display of shilly-shallying, perhaps *you* will demonstrate the character required to use *alright* to pollute the pure waters of Good English, not accepting that its place is solely in the muddy puddles of common usage.

Nother is another premium non-word, despised but persistent, particularly identified with the phrase 'a whole nother'. So contemptible is it taken to be, so low, that the friendly arbiters of

---

* Actually, before *lonely*, English did have the adjective *elenge*. (In *Right Word, Wrong Word*, V. H. Collins argues that in the sentence 'He was all alone', the word *all* is superfluous and 'should be omitted'. For more on pleonasm, see Chapter 17.)

proper usage whom we have so far met in this book do not even mention it. (What, you might justly wonder, does this tell us about the status of the hated forms they *do* mention?)

The phrase 'a whole nother' is a good example of what linguists call 'metanalysis' or 'false splitting': the word *another* is made from *an* plus *other*, but after a 'false' split, the *n* from *an* has migrated. Because 'a whole nother' is widely used in spoken English, it also now shows up on the page. In David Foster Wallace's novel of 1996, *Infinite Jest*, a character sleeps against one wall, but wakes to find the bed 'against a whole nother wall'.* Would a griper instead say 'a whole other'? No. If our authorities had deigned to address themselves to this question, they would probably have proposed 'a different X', 'a completely different X', or 'another X entirely'. But why?

After all, and as ever, there are words in English arrived at by the same means as *nother* that the starchiest of gripers accept, use and even enjoy. They might spurn an apron, disavow a nickname or shudder at the humble newt, but they do not object to the fact that the words *apron*, *nickname* and *newt* were formed by metanalysis—a *newt* having once been an *ewt*; an *apron*, a *napron*; a *nickname*, an *eke* or 'also' name. And what of the word *umpire*, another example, once *noumpere*, derived from the Old French *nonper*, meaning 'without peer'? Does it really matter if such words drift into the language—or that they sometimes drift out again? Anyone familiar with *King Lear* will recall that Shakespeare had his *nuncles*—*nuncle* being a form that arose from a mis-splitting of *mine uncle*. *Nuncle*, and its pair, *naunt*, have not remained in widespread use. And the label *nidiot* has gone too—for a long

---

* Wallace knew exactly what he was up to when he wrote this. In his 2001 essay 'Tense Present: Democracy, English, and the Wars over Usage', he amply proved himself to have internalised the sensibilities of what he called the language 'snoot'.

time *nidiot* was a variant form of *idiot*. For a while it was even boiled down to *nigit*. Was *that* to be reviled?

Nother, it so happens, is a very old word. It can be found in *Beowulf*, around the year 1000, where it is used to mean 'neither'. And in the fifteenth century, the excellent phrase *neither nother* arose to mean 'neither one thing nor the other'. But the earliest citation given by the *OED* for the exact sense found in the expression 'a whole nother' dates to around 1375, appearing in a quotation where the writer exclaims: my sight is servant to my heart '& alle my noþer wolnk wittes' (i.e. '& all my nother excellent senses'). In short, *nother* has been lurking about in the vocabulary of English for many hundreds of years, for most of this span meaning 'other'. Yet what are the chances of its ever being accepted in this guise by our gripers?

They perhaps hope that the expression 'a whole nother' is where the rough handling of *another* begins and ends today. If so, this hope—like so many of their hopes—is going unanswered. Take, for example, the advertising slogan 'Want a(nother) tattoo?' In formal English this means 'Would you like a tattoo, or—should you have one already—another tattoo?' It cannot be denied that 'a(nother)' is deft; that translating it into formal English produces a sentence that is not deft; and that to say 'Want a/another tattoo?' would sound worse than either. And if that seems to be a special case, consider that other *nother*s out there in everyday exchanges are being shown the respect of the definite article, as in 'The only nother minor complaint is the pitch of the motor'. Clearly *nother* is fighting hard for its place in the language. But that is not a reason for you to leave its fate to chance. As long as the naysayers implicitly declare, 'While we have *other*, we recognise no *nother*', an advanced misuser of English must stand up for this redoubtable little word.

II

SYNCOPE; MUMBLING; MANGLING

deteriate, euw, infatic

Having looked at how to lose bits of words in the act of combining two or more, let us now turn to those words that get squished, squashed and otherwise messed about with singly.

In the last chapter, we glancingly met 'aphesis' and 'apocope', where lexical matter disappears from the front or back of a word. When bits slip out of the middle, this is known in the trade as 'syncope', giving us, for example, *bosun* from *boatswain*, *jetsam* from *jettison*, and *innards* from *inwards* (the *OED*, in need of revision here, describes *innards* as a 'Dial. and vulgar alteration').

So far, these days, so acceptable. But what about this: 'the city began coming to life: men yelling, their words untelligible', or 'To someone not familiar with computer systems, that sentence is as untelligible as "The mome raths outgrabe"'?* What of the person who writes helpfully that silicates in car-engine coolants 'will deteriate your water pump seals'? In October of 1834, *The Westminster Review* characterised *deteriate* as just the sort of 'scrap' those ignorant of Latin sometimes 'catch from the lips of their superiors in education': implicitly, the ignorant have half-heard and are now misspelling a word whose utility they deduced from

---

* Ken McGoogan, *Chasing Safiya*, 1999, pp. 118–19; Allan D. Pratt, *The Information of the Image*, 1982, p. 9.

hearing it correctly used by the educated. In 1926, Henry Watson Fowler also warned his readers about *deteriate* in his *Dictionary of Modern English Usage*. No doubt he would be wearily unsurprised to learn that it has not gone away: 'economic conditions had deteriated'; 'Ground glitter and other sources may deteriate the signals and their information contents'; 'There is an irreversible downward trend ultimately at work in our universe where everything is deteriating'.*

Those who remain faithful to *unintelligible* and *deteriorate* will hardly be foxed by the quotations above; but as the compacted versions of these words become increasingly widespread, they will inevitably cause ever more gripers to fret and fume. Indeed, the merest suspicion of syncope, with its threatening taint of 'inferior' speech, is liable to give any true griper the horrors. Simon Heffer wrongly blames *specialty* on the Americans and declares that substituting *specialty* for *speciality* in British English is 'pretentious or just silly'. For what it is worth, the word *specialty* has been bouncing around in English since long before America, as we now know it, had any English to corrupt—since 1330, to be precise; *speciality* did not come in until a century or more afterwards. Similarly, the word *adaption* worries many of our advisers. Kingsley Amis conceded that compared with *adaptation*, the short form seemed 'sensible', but he feared the 'imputation of illiteracy' if he should use it. The commentator R. H. Fiske more crudely rules that *adaption* is 'misused' for *adaptation*. He is right—again: for what it is worth—that, here, the word *adaptation* came first, according to the researches of the *OED*. He is right, but as *adaption* and *adaptation* both sprang into being during the back end

---

* Roy Dutton, *Financial Meltdown*, 2009, p. 58; Ehrhard Raschke, in *Radiation and Water in the Climate System*, Raschke (ed.), 1996, p. 23; Charles Sykes, *People of God*, 2005, p. 129.

of the life of Shakespeare, whether syncope strictly applies is hard to say.

Before you run away with the idea that sticking to the shortest form of a word will give you your best chance of irritating the gripers, see how Mr Fiske goes to town on *orientate*, deriding it as more 'unwieldy and cacophonic than the less syllabic *orient*'. Some single words are taken to have been squished and squashed; others, to have had unnecessary bits trippingly added on or in. If Mr Fiske's criticism is valid, why he did not describe the more syllabic *adaptation* as 'cacophonic' too is anyone's guess. The short-form *preventive* is similarly recommended by him—as also by Bill Bryson—over the boggy *preventative*. (Ambrose Bierce wrote confidently in 1909, 'No such word as preventative'; Richard Grant White, in 1870, that use of *preventative* was evidence 'of an utter want of education and of a low grade of intelligence'.) Both forms date from the seventeenth century; they came into use within about three decades of each other. Meanwhile, all defenders of Good English loathe, detest and abhor *mischievious*. The shorter *mischievous* came into English in the late fourteenth century, when it meant 'impoverished' and 'depressed'. But since the seventeenth century, it has been spelt by some and no doubt also pronounced as though akin to *devious*, a longer form that has been widespread now for a couple of hundred years. A 1799 report on the slave trade, presented to the House of Commons, speaks of 'the machinations of mischievious emissaries'; and there are many nineteenth-century editions of the works of writers from Bunyan to Gibbon that contain the expanded version of the word.

What might be characterised by some as sloppiness of speech becomes, in extreme form, mumbling. And though the image of a mumbler is these days associated in particular with drunkards, anyone shy and those adolescents who seem almost to desire to be misunderstood (perhaps for the pleasure of feeling persecuted), indistinct speech has a long religious history too. In some medieval Mystery Plays, the character of Titivil, a devil with a net, was dedicated to gathering up words mismanaged or lost during church services. These he took away to Hell to preserve as evidence against the mumbling offender. The lost word *overhip* meant to skip or 'over-hop' words entirely: a book of four sermons printed by Caxton in 1483 warns its readers against 'ouerhippyng ne momblyng'. Also dating from the fifteenth century is the compound *pitter-patter*, the earliest meaning of which was the too-speedy and by extension the senseless recital of prayers. In eighteenth-century editions of Francis Grose's *Classical Dictionary of the Vulgar Tongue*, after the verb *hum* is defined as meaning both 'hesitate' (as in *hum and haw*), and 'deceive' (as in *humbug*), it is explained to the reader that 'a great number of hums' in church has the slang meaning 'a large congregation', while a *hum box* is a pulpit.

What these old uses share is implied censure, from various angles, of those suspected of not having quite meant what they managed not quite to say—but should have said, and meant. We do, however, often communicate sense by deliberately inarticulate means. Because many great writers have tried to invoke authentic-seeming speech on the page, great literature is a wonderful source of what the gripers might call sub-literate expression. According to the *OED*, Shakespeare gave us *hoo*; Byron, *bah*; Thackeray, *h'm*, *pfui*, *shshsh* and *yoop*; George Eliot, *tchu* and *pst*; James Joyce, *uff*. And there are many other such 'interjections', as they are rather flatly labelled, that have become conventional. The startled *ha* is dated by the *OED* to about 1320 and the interrogative *um*, to 1672, while the assenting *mm* suddenly appears in 1911. All these and many more—*oh*, *ah*, *whoops*, *ugh*, *wow*, and so on—are now part of ordinary English discourse. A strikingly early attempt to pin down one or two of these suggestive sounds, found in a Latin Grammar composed by the Benedictine abbot

Ælfric in about the year 1000 (unusually for the time, written in the vernacular), explains that 'ha ha and he he getacniaþ hlehter on leden and on englisc' ('*ha ha* and *he he* signify laughter in Latin and in English'). We have our own, modern interjections too, naturally disliked by our reeling gripers. To invoke those important human staples indifference, contempt and dismay, numerous people have now slipped into using *meh*, *duh* and variations on *euw* (*ew*, *ewww*, *euww*)—threatening to leave earlier forms like *pshaw*, *phooey* and *yikes* in the shade.

In *Don't*, a renowned 1883 manual by 'Censor' that offers advice on 'Mistakes & Improprieties more or less prevalent in Conduct and Speech', the author writes: 'Don't mangle your words, or smother them, or swallow them', and 'Don't use meaningless exclamations, such as "Oh, my!" "Oh, crackey!", etc.' Scholars dedicated to what they call 'discourse analysis' try to carve up truly smothered and mangled communication into different kinds. The label 'non-lexical back channels' is sometimes given to those noises we make—*hn?*, *mnmn*—when, rather than give a reply, we merely want to persuade the people talking to us that we are interested in what they have to say—which perhaps we are! 'Phatic communion', meanwhile, covers the phenomenon of words spoken without reference to their literal meaning—as when 'how's things' functions as a salute and not a question. But for our purposes, those good old catch-alls *mumbling* and *mangling* will do, providing a great realm of imprecision where dreaded non-words are occasionally born.

Shakespeare has his clowns, mechanicals and pot-house folk use 'allicholly' to mean *melancholy*, 'argall' to mean *ergo*, and 'haber de poiz' to mean *avoirdupois* (selling by weight). In *Mill on the Floss*, George Eliot has Maggie play 'marls' as a child, not *marbles*. There is a wilful, jokey muddle when James Joyce has a character in *Ulysses* say 'weggebobble' for *vegetable*, or when Kipling, in 1896, supplies this corruption of *hermaphrodite*: "E's a kind of a giddy harumfrodite—soldier an'sailor too!' Our advisers approach such mangling with anticipatory relish when it is dished up to them by a solid literary genius. Otherwise not. In a lost corner of the *OED*, *ingram* is boldly defined as 'a perverted form' of *ignorant*. *The Economist Style Guide* says sniffily that although use of *wannabes* should be limited, it 'should not be banned', as though it could be. The daily despairers grind their teeth over those who text *imma* to mean 'I'm going to', or who write of 'a book I've read dunamany times already',* or who, in commissioned prose, inflict apocope on the word *biased*: 'A central west magistrate has rejected claims he is bias against the Aboriginal Legal Service' (ABC News). But a word the gripers will hate even more than these from the very first moment they encounter it is *infatic*: 'The 1st real test of the season saw Portsmouth respond with an infatic victory over previous level peggers Gosport' (Portsmouth Cricket Club, match report, June 2008). If you are asking yourself whether, given the existence of 'infatic' victories, there are also now ordinary folk who, seeking to draw attention to this or that, *infasise* it—well, there are: 'Due to some confusion last time we would like to infasise that this is a Sunday afternoon show ...'.

In short, there is junking odd bits of words, and there is needlessly adding extra bits on or in—and by such moves the language has gained vocabulary that even its most conservative users consider legitimate. Yet if you venture outside the bounds of what those conservative users call Good English, expect to be condemned for your 'utter want of education and low grade of intelligence'. If you *adoptate*† even one or two horrible examples—possibly words that have been in the language for

---

* For more on text-speak, see Chapter 21.
† '... the term "ultimate disposal" is a misnomer, but is included here because of its adoptation by the EPA': Brent Wainwright and Louis Theodore, in *Pollution Prevention*, Theodore, Dupont and Reynolds (eds.), 1994, p. 2.

centuries—you will be received as a victim of the attractive ignorance of others, feebly *co-opted** into an attack on what is correct. Worse, if you *infasise* words that are being positively and severely mangled, you will be accused of trading in nonsense. But then, is nonsense really so dreadful? In a letter of 1898, Conrad wrote despairingly, 'Half the words we use have no meaning whatever and of the other half each man understands each word after the fashion of his own folly and conceit'. To this one can only respond that, if so, we get by remarkably well. And anyway, even when English *is* cut with manifest nonsense, that nonsense can be highly communicative—as *The Poor Soldier*, a comic opera from the late eighteenth century, shows:

> The cock courts his hens all around me,
> The sparrow, the pigeon, and dove;
> Oh! how all this courtship confounds me,
> For want of the girl that I love!
> Dootherum, doodle-adgity, nadgety, tragedy, rum,
> Gooseterum, foodle-igity, fidgety, nidgety, mum.

* '… the democratic "revolution" and its co-optation by late capitalism' (*Mail and Guardian*). (In the past, *co-optate* meant, not 'co-opt', but 'choose'.)

12
BABY TALK

ouchie

The fastidious reader sighing over a distorted word may well be looking at a form committed to the page by a writer innocently unaware of the regular alternative. In a different class altogether are the distorters of words who go about their task on purpose. These people no doubt cause annoyance with their every wayward locution. And yet of all the motives for deliberately interfering with the usual forms of our words, there is one that reigns supreme in the dismay it inspires—a dismay so profound that anyone might feel it, griper or not. This motive is the wish, broadly speaking, to render one's language infantile.

On 21 April 1711, Addison wrote in *The Spectator*:

> A very ingenious *French* Author tells us, that the Ladies of the Court of *France*, in his Time, thought it ill-breeding, and a kind of Female Pedantry, to pronounce an hard Word right; for which Reason they took frequent occasion to use hard Words, that they might shew Politeness in murdering them. He further adds, that a Lady of some Quality at Court, having accidentally made use of an hard Word in a proper Place, and pronounced it right, the whole Assembly was out of Countenance for her.

This story reflects badly on the men who accepted such tributes, and about as badly on the women who offered them. Availing oneself of 'hard Words' merely to pull off a silly-little-me act seems nauseating. Still, that was the point.

Among English speakers, those under similar pressure to pass themselves off as inferior need hardly go to such lengths. Much the same effect can be created without study by faking a lisp.* Nor is there an obvious cost in anything but grated nerves when a person uses 'hypocoristic' or 'pet' names, or, put another way, descends into baby language. In grated nerves, however, the cost can be quite tremendous.

The *OED* credits Jane Austen with the first recorded use of *itty* as a shortening. One hopes, rather a lot, that there was an affectionate touch of irony to her words in a letter of 1798 when she wrote, about her nephew 'little George', 'I flatter myself that *itty Dordy* will not forget me'. Fifty years later, Dickens, in *Dombey and Son*, seems to have had qualms after getting Mrs Chick to say, 'I thought I should have fallen out of the staircase window as I came down from seeing dear Fanny, and that tiddy ickle sing'. A narrative passage hastily explains: 'These last words originated in a sudden vivid reminiscence of the baby'. Mrs Chick's unexpected mental flip-flop has sent her to *tiddy* for 'small', or perhaps 'tiny', to *ickle* for *little*, and *sing* for *thing*, in a stab at matching the untuned speech of an 'ickle' child.† A crueller picture of such sentimentalising occurs in George Orwell's novel of 1936, *Keep the Aspidistra Flying*, in which he imagines a genteel lady in a library 'enthusing' over a book of dog photographs: 'a Peke, the ickle angel pet, wiv his gweat big Soulful eyes and his ickle black nosie—oh so ducky-duck!' Presumably most people overhearing

---

* The French do also lisp. The French verbs for lisping—*zézayer* and, less formally, *zozoter*—are rare examples in that tongue of onomatopoeia.
† This is not to suggest that Dickens was the first to use these shortenings. For instance, *The Universal Songster, or Museum of Mirth*, Vol. III, 1826, illustrated by the Cruikshanks, Robert and George, contains a ditty under the title 'Ickle Chicka Happy Squad Wid a Jolly Tar'.

this sort of talk in a library would find themselves wishing for a sick bag.

Many scholars believe that using this kind of cooing baby talk in an attempt to nurture speech in the very young is sensible and good—and that it works. There are, however, further motives for deploying such vocabulary that have nothing to do with promoting language-acquisition in 'tiddy ickle sings'.

One is flirtation. The word *ducky*, used in Orwell's line of drivel above, first enters the records of English in the writings of Henry VIII, who used it in a letter to Anne Boleyn as a pet term for her breasts: 'wishing my self (specially an Evening) in my Sweethearts Armes', he confessed, 'whose pritty Duckys I trust shortly to kysse'. He finished, 'Writne with the Hand of him that was, is, and shall be yours by his will, H R', and soon after had her beheaded. In a conventional account, those who use baby language to flirt cast themselves in either a needy or a protecting role, but the transaction has the potential to be far subtler, surely, than this. When in December 2013 a law court broadcast several voicemail messages of the man second in line to the British throne, messages illegally intercepted in 2006 by the *News of the World*, newspaper after newspaper chose to report the story under a headline that featured his use, in addressing the then Miss Middleton, of the pet name *babykins*. Though these headlines had a sheen of prurience to them, the word *babykins* itself was deemed by instant analysts of the Prince's verbal style to be blameless.* What interested reporters about the nickname was not that a possible future queen was being infantilised, but that a probable future king had it in him to be so comfortably silly.

---

* The diminutive suffix *-kin* is hundreds of years old. Shakespeare used *lamkin*, 'little lamb', to describe a young man, while one female equivalent of the period was *minikin*.

Modern commentators have, however, been squeamish about more extreme use of such language by figures of note from the past. It is difficult to plumb the relationship between Jonathan Swift, scourge of those whom he despised, and Esther Johnson, whom he called 'Stella'. They first met when he was twenty-two and she was eight. Her parentage was a mystery, but she had protectors. Swift, in need of money, accepted the job of being her tutor. They were thereafter closely and affectionately caught up with each other until she died in 1728, aged forty-six. After Swift himself died, letters he had written to her between 1710 and 1713 were published under the title *Journal to Stella*. Swift, we know, because he says so, took Esther Johnson's letters to bed with him, but more than that it is impossible to say. Letters from her to him have not survived. Much of the content of his to her is political gossip, but his writing also contains many examples, some undecipherable, of what he called their 'little language'. She is not only 'saucy sluttikins' and 'Ppt' for *poppet*, but 'ung oomens', as well. Swift uses 'iss I tan, well as oo' for 'yes I can, as well as you', 'dood mollow' for 'good morrow', and many other pseudo-artless approximations. At one point he explains: 'when I am writing in our language I make up my mouth just as if I was speaking it'. Elsewhere he takes (false) comfort from the idea that their habit of communicating like this will make their writing invulnerable to the gaze of a hostile world: 'a bad scrawl is so snug'.

Swift would later be more than matched in this correspondence by John Ruskin, whose liking for a far younger girl is also not our real subject here. But—once more with a notional sick bag to hand—consider that Ruskin, in his fifties, was keen to write to his much younger cousin Joan, 'Me dedful tired and worrited', while reflecting quite correctly that people might be 'dedfu socked 'at we tant pell any betty'. Later he would refer to this language as his 'baby misbinefs'. When he was especially unkeen on being in Oxford, he wrote to her saying, 'me so dismal me don't no fot to do.— Me want to give up bein Pefsor'.*

Thomas Nashe appears a good deal more straightforward in dashing off playfully, in 1596, 'because she is such a hony sweetikin, let her bee *Prick-madam*'. Yet no one who dips into this subject can resist quoting Thackeray's impressive take on Swift's 'little language': 'I know of nothing more manly, more tender, more exquisitely touching'. Who are we to say, with the disadvantages of hindsight, what was really going on in the souls of those most concerned? For present purposes, what we need to bear in mind is no more than the likely effect of such writing on the casual outsider of today. And to that, the answer is simple: today's casual outsider will almost certainly feel repelled.

Though a sprinkling of baby language may convey its users into the realm of coy flirtation, these forms can also be used— flirtatiously or otherwise—to veil indelicate subjects. *Piddle* has been a childish word for urinating since the late eighteenth century, though with other meanings the verb is much older. *Tummy* from *stomach*, and the lavatorial use of *poop*, are both Victorian. From the twentieth century, we have *potty* as a nursery word for *chamber pot*, and *icky*, a portmanteau word derived from *sickly* and *sticky*, and so on. Given that baby talk is implicitly hierarchical, it can also be deployed to convey contempt. Notoriously, when in 1928 Dorothy Parker, as 'Constant Reader', reviewed A. A. Milne's *The House at Pooh Corner* for the *New Yorker*, she wrote that his word *hummy* marked the first place 'at which Tonstant Weader fwowed up'. In fact, some babyish words are almost always employed to negative effect. From the 1890s, *diddums*—i.e. 'did thems' mistreat you?—is resolutely unkind; and from 1905 *twee*, a childlike rendering of *sweet*, is, in the delivery, rarely approving.

* See Rachel Dickinson (ed.), *John Ruskin's Correspondence with Joan Severn*, 2009.

In all this, what of the babies themselves? Percival Leigh, in his *Comic English Grammar* of 1840, wrote, 'The vocal comicalities of the infant in arms are exceedingly laughable,* but we are unfortunately unable to spell them'. This was to give up too easily. An infant in arms generally moves from simple babbling to what specialists call 'reduplicative† babbling', found in such uses as *mama, dada, wee wee* and *boo boo*; it is no accident that in our second childhood we are at risk of becoming 'gaga'. The reduplicative phase of baby babblesque is mirrored in such nursery staples as the characters *baa baa* black sheep, *incy wincy* spider, *Chicken Licken* and *Humpty Dumpty*; in *choo choo* trains and the *nimble namble* riding game; in the adjectives *teeny-weeny, easy-peasy*, and the like.

But this seemingly childish lexical mannerism is found in ordinary adult vocabulary too. English has a vast number of what are called 'reduplicative compounds', where either the vowels alter: *dilly-dally, wishy-washy, zigzag, flip-flop*—or the consonants: *hurly-burly, helter-skelter, hoity-toity, willy-nilly*. Many writers have been inspired to create their own examples. Shakespeare wrote of 'skimble skamble' stuff, meaning disorderly nonsense. Fanny Burney, in 1778, invented *skimper scamper* to mean 'confusedly'. Keats, in the early nineteenth century, dreamt up *ruffy-tuffy* to mean 'dishevelled', and H. G. Wells in 1910 coined *pitter-litter*. This was supposed to invoke tumbling down the stairs, but what he meant when he also wrote, in 1937, of 'the wimble-wamble of the common world', no one has been able to say.

Reduplicative compounds do not always come across as childlike, but so strong is their association with childish speech that it would be hard to concoct a new example that had gravitas right

---

* By *laughable* Leigh meant, not 'risible', but 'funny'. Leigh is now remembered—if at all—as a peripheral figure in the circle of Charles Dickens.
† *Reduplicate*, like *duplicate*, means 'duplicate'.

off the bat.* In a scene in his 1918 novel *Joan and Peter*, Wells, who appears to have had a special fondness for the form, depicts a delinquent aunt trying to manoeuvre two innocent little children into allowing themselves to be christened. She points out to them seductively her 'croquet-poky lawn', and a pony wearing 'booty-pootys' so as not to harm the grass while it pulls a mower. Then she tries to tempt them into what she vilely calls the 'churchy-perchy'. She speaks of 'all sorts of things', says Wells, before adding savagely, 'Particularly the churchy-perchy'.

He was not the first to use a reduplicative compound to convey this degree of disdain for an adult. What we now think of as the adjective *namby-pamby* started out as an insulting nickname for the mediocre eighteenth-century poet Ambrose Philips. Philips's great enemy was Pope, who referred to him as 'Namby Pamby' in *The Dunciad*; but the compound first found its way into print courtesy of Henry Carey in his scathing parody of Philips's infantile rhyming: '*Namby-Pamby*'s doubly Mild, / Once a Man, and twice a Child ... Now he Pumps his little Wits, / Sh—ing Writes, and Writing Sh—ts, / All by little tiny Bits ...' (there is much more of this). With such a festival of derision behind it, the expression *namby-pamby*, in the general sense of 'sentimentally insipid', soon took off, so that by 1766, Richard Griffith, in a letter to his wife (the literary pair we met in Chapter 3), could call any sort of lowering of the tone in addressing a child 'Namby Pambicks'.

Three hundred years after Ambrose Philips was in his heyday, namby-pambicising is with us still. A notorious recent example occurred in a 2007 episode of *Doctor Who*, 'Blink'. With the

---

* Ruskin, in his troubling letters to Joan Severn, used 'tipsywipsy' to mean drunk, 'growly wowly' for ill temper, 'munchy-unchy-punchy' for lunch, and 'misby-thisby-misby' for utterly miserable. He called her 'Joanie Ponie', 'Doaneyky Poneyky', 'Pussky Mussky', 'itie Fitie', 'Poosmoos', and more.

combined time-travel stories of series upon series threatening to make even an amateur logician cry, David Tennant was called on to explain away the madness that had been generated by successive writers. He did so by saying that time is not linear, but must be thought of as 'a big ball of wibbly-wobbly timey-wimey stuff'. Come the 2014 Christmas special, Santa Claus (or a projection of Santa Claus) would ridicule the flustered Time Lord (now played by Peter Capaldi) for the feeble quality of his scientific explanations: 'As the Doctor might say, "Oh, it's all a bit dreamy-weamy"'.

It may by this point be striking you that no one sane would risk speaking publicly in baby language, even to a baby. And certainly the limits are tight on what anyone but an extremist considers its acceptable uses. There are a few old, well-established forms that seem to pass muster, such as Swift's 'up a-dazy', now *upsidaisy*, from 1711, or *beddy-byes*, which sounds cheery enough. To balance these, there are new forms likely to inspire particularly keen dislike. The small child of today who has taken a topple, and who sits with arms outstretched weeping 'uppie',* may well be viewed unkindly by a sensitive passer-by. Unbearable will be the grown-up who comforts the forlorn child by discussing its *ouchie*.†

The good news for your campaign is that if you ever get tired of the niceties of battle, and want nothing more than to throw bricks for a spell, the slightest trace of baby talk should render your English repulsive in almost every circumstance. The bad news is that in reaching for this weapon you risk disgusting yourself. And now, let us with inestimable relief move on.

---

* Literally and metaphorically, 'pick me up'.
† '... if you have an ouchie and your mind goes crazy ... you may very well turn an ouchie into a blister': see Michael Sky, *Dancing with the Fire*, 2011, p. 159. Some people prefer the form *owie*—a word that has made it into the *OED*.

13

AFFIXES

innuendous

So far in this book we have looked at misinterpreting, reimagining, mashing together, mangling, multiplying and generally messing about with various words. In the process, we have rather skipped over those conventional elements, unable to stand as words in their own right, that get added on to words at their beginnings or ends.* These elements are referred to as 'prefixes' when they go at the front and 'suffixes' when they go at the back, and are jointly known as 'affixes'.† In Chapter 4, we saw how *-ize* and *-ise* could turn existing words of several kinds into verbs: *incentivise*, *smallise*, *otherise*; and we have just seen how the diminutive suffixes *-y* and *-ikin* can be used to create endearments such as *ducky* and *sweetikin*. Now that we are coming to look at this topic more closely, it is necessary to mention that prefixes and suffixes are divided by linguists into several disputed sub-categories. But here we have no need to worry about that.

English would be hamstrung without the word-altering possibilities of affixes. Their use goes all the way back to the known

---

* Linguists refer to them for this reason as 'bound' elements (as mentioned on p. 61), though see p. 31 for an exception, the prefix *dis-*, now widely used as an informal verb to *diss*.

† Not all linguists would agree about this, but the *OED* explains the word *outright* as being a prefix prefixed to a suffix, if you ever wondered whether such a thing might be possible.

origins of the language. Consider the effects of a few of them on *diore*, our word *dear*, an adjective in English from the ninth century on. Originally *diore* meant glorious, noble, what is viewed with tenderness or love, and that which is valuable—either expensive to buy, or 'dear to the heart'. In Old English it had its own opposite by way of the negative prefix *un-*: *undeor* was used to mean commonplace, cheap or unvalued—before in the fourteenth century this word slipped out of the language. The loss of *undeor* contrasts with the fate of *diorling*, meaning 'dearling' or *darling*. The suffix *-ling*, joined to an adjective, indicates that somebody or something possesses the quality of that adjective. A *iungling* or 'youngling' used to mean a young person; an *efenling* or 'evenling', an equal or a neighbour; an *irpling* or 'earthling', a ploughman; and so on. The word *darling*, as it now is, has been a treasured resource for speakers of English from the ninth century on. But *dear* took a very different path when, in the thirteenth century, it was given the suffix *-th*. Added to an adjective, *-th* yields a noun: by this means the Old English words *mirige* (*merry*), *ful* (*foul*), *lang* (*long*) and *treowe* (*true*), gave *mirigþ* (*mirth*), *fylþ* (*filth*), *lengþ* (*length*) and *triewþ* (*truth*).* There was at first pressure to make *dearth*, 'dearness', mean glory or splendour. But the association of *dear* with high values, and by extension with scarcity, meant that *dearth* took hold to much greater effect, then and thereafter, as a word for deprivation and lack.

Many Old English words take several affixes at once. For example, from *eape*, meaning 'ease' (though *ease* and *eape* are unrelated), came the noun *uneaðelicness*, an 'un-*eape*-like-ness', or, roughly, a 'difficulty'; and *forepancfull* combined the idea of *forepanc* or 'forethought' and *pancfull* or 'thoughtful' to produce the beguiling adjective 'forethoughtful'. Anyone can try sticking

---

* The Middle English word *triews* or *truce*, a covenant of good faith, derives from the plural form *truths*.

an affix on to a word to alter its meaning and purpose. The compound adjective *brainsick* had been in the English language for several centuries when Shakespeare, wanting it for an adverb in *Macbeth*, stuck *-ly* to the end: 'To think / So brainsickly of things'. He did the same with the noun *cannibal* in *Coriolanus*: 'And he had been cannibally given, he might have broiled and eaten him too'. These two adverbs have been little fancied by the masses since, but their construction is impeccable.

Even when impeccable construction is wedded to a needed and welcome sense, this is not necessarily enough to secure a word in the language, as there is also fashion to worry about. We no longer say *ill-willy* to mean *ill-willed*, or *careful* to mean 'grief-stricken'. A high Victorian work such as George Eliot's last novel, *Daniel Deronda*, will provide numerous instances of affixes used to generate words that are now outmoded. Flicking through just a few of its pages, we find that she writes *greenth* rather than *greenery*, *suspensive* rather than *suspenseful*, *duteous* rather than *dutiful*, *troublous* rather than *troublesome*, *tumultuary* rather than *tumultuous*, and *scathless* rather than *unscathed*. She uses *anecdotic* to mean 'full of anecdote', *dubitatively* to mean 'doubtfully', and *relishing* to mean 'pleasurable': 'if his puddings were rolling towards him in the dust, he took the inside bits and found them relishing'. We may judge these words to be 'relishing' too, but they would not go down smoothly in modern English prose.

Seeming passé is not the only reason the use of a given affix might come over as incongruous. Our beliefs, almost certainly unexamined, about the fittingness of each for different purposes allow for humour when a writer deliberately strays from convention. The nineteenth-century label an *indifferentist* sounds fairly frigid. An earlier term for the same character-type, used by Swift but not invented by him, is an *anythingarian*, which sounds far sillier, perhaps because it mixes the Latin *-arian* with the humdrum, Old English *anything*—a word that dates back to around 700. The great eighteenth-century figure Horace Walpole (whose cat died in Chapter 1) was also fond of this sort of fun. In a letter of 1752 that goes on to make an accusation of incest, he writes humorously to a friend, 'I am glad you are aware of Miss Pitt; pray continue your awaredom'. He also coined the words *gloomth*, *snubee*, *nabobical*, *incumbentess* and *robberaciously* (which piles suffix upon suffix). In all cases, Walpole slyly mocked whatever he was writing about by devising a word for it that seemed faintly ridiculous.

The considerable choice we have in how to achieve a particular meaning with one or another affix, the potential nevertheless for the meaning of the resulting word to become a matter of dispute, and the fact that the choice of added element is in part a matter of fashion—all of this means that there is an enormous amount of room for perceived *misuse* of affixes. There was, for example, a long-fought battle over the word *restive* by those who wanted it to suggest something like 'at rest'. Ambrose Bierce, in 1909, wrote the following bitter remark about the mixing-up of *restive* and *restless*: 'These words have directly contrary meanings; the dictionaries' disallowance of their identity would be something to be thankful for, but that is a dream'. Poor old Whitten and Whitaker, in *Good and Bad English*, were still troubled by this in 1946. It happens, however, that *restive* has meant both 'inactive' and 'restless' from the start (i.e. from around 1550), for the strikingly specific reason that a 'restive' or supposedly stationary quadruped, in particular a horse, especially when positively refusing to be driven forwards, is liable to dance about sideways and even backwards rather than simply standing still.

In 1877, Fitzedward Hall, a scholar interested in 'lingual detrition at its extreme limit', and a great contributor to the *OED*,

wrote an entire book on '*Reliable* and words similar'.* Richard
Grant White, a few years earlier, had described *reliable* as 'ignorantly formed by the union of incongruous elements'. Many of
his English counterparts wrongly assumed that it was a recent
Americanism (the *OED* dates it back to a Scottish text of 1569),
and some blamed its growing popularity in Victorian England
on 'our dreadful cockneys'. A critic for *The Saturday Review* in
1875 wrote that an Englishman 'supposed to have been educated'
who 'can bring himself to use, we cannot say the word, for it is
not a word, but that absurd and stupid vulgarism, *reliable*, must
have a screw loose somewhere'.† The argument about *reliable* as
expressed by this critic went beyond describing it as awkwardly
put together, to the assertion that a 'reliable person' should mean
'a person who is *able to rely*' and not 'a person who is *capable of
being relied upon*'. To cap it all, there was the fear that it would
displace *trustworthy*, not merely a splendid word, the naysayers
felt, but one that meant just what it looked as though it ought
to mean.

Yet *-able* had been used in the disputed fashion in English so
widely and for so long that the tide of criticism against *reliable*
seems perverse. What of *dependable* (depend-*on*-able), *laughable*
(laugh-*at*-able), *unthinkable* (unthink-*about*-able)? These no more
posed a problem then than they do now. And A. P. Herbert must
have come across as positively recherché when he wrote in
1935 that he detested the use of *knowledgeable* to describe one
who has knowledge, rather than one able to acquire it. (The first

---

* See *On English Adjectives in -Able: With Special Reference to Reliable*, 1877.
† These two quotations were drawn by Fitzedward Hall from *The Literary
Churchman*, 1860, p. 442, and *The Saturday Review*, 1875, p. 795. Fitzedward
Hall himself dismissed as 'insolent' the 'screw-loose' argument against *reliable*
(*reliable* referred to by him as 'the word reprobated').

meaning given to the word *knowledgeable* was actually 'recognisable' or 'knowable', but on this he had nothing to say.)

Granted, there are examples of adjectives formed with *-able* that have changed meaning over time, acquiring an implicit preposition along the way. If we say that a house is barely *liveable*, we mean it is barely 'live-*in*-able'—a sense of the word first given to the language by Jane Austen in *Mansfield Park*. Before this, *liveable* meant 'capable of life', or, as an infant at birth is sometimes said to be, 'viable'. (NB Bill Bryson declares that *viable* 'does not mean feasible or workable or promising'. True, one wants to reply—except on the countless occasions when it *does*.) *Liveable* as 'live-*in*-able' is now fully accommodated in English, but what of *relatable*? Before 1950, *relatable* on its own meant 'able to be related', as a pious but not a bawdy story might be *relatable* before the Queen. However, since the 1960s, and with gathering momentum, its sense has been changing, so that free advice given to the monarchy recently via CNN—that it needs to be 'distant but relatable'—is intended to suggest, not prim mythologising from afar, but the idea that the monarchy should be, while dignified, 'relate-*to*-able'—a meaning of the word that makes today's gripers wince.

English is still throwing up *-able* words on the griper-approved pattern, such as *biodegradable*, meaning, crudely, 'able to be decomposed by living organisms'. But *-able* is a suffix so beguiling that it will never be limited to this one use, as witness the new and exciting non-word *bigable*, used in a copy-shop slogan: 'Photos are bigable with a click'.

With *reliable* and *restive*, as we now know them, having won their place in Good English at last, American gripers have been left to worry instead about the interpretation of *nauseous*, a pointless difficulty that Mr Bryson wishes to import into British English. When someone says 'Harold is nauseous', should this be taken to mean that Harold causes nausea in others or is suffering from it himself? As the suffix *-ous* generally means 'full of' or 'abounding in', there are some words, such as *noxious*, that might be taken to support the first interpretation, and others, such as *obsequious*, the second. Yet a word like *suspicious* can go both ways without this seeming to matter to anyone ('he appeared suspicious': either 'he appeared to be suspicious about X' or 'he was viewed by Y with suspicion'). In short, there is no right answer, and it is all a matter of context. Mr Bryson rules loftily that in Harold's case, if he feels sick, 'Make it *nauseated*'; but popular usage in England does nothing to clinch his little nicety. *The Economist Style Guide*, meanwhile, with overweening scrupulosity, declares that *finally* should not be used to mean 'at last', but 'for the last time'—as though the sentence 'The shift workers finally ate' ought to be taken to imply that, after the meal in question, the wretched shift workers never ate again.

We have seen that our gripers can be narrow in how they pick their hate-words, directing their animus at a limited hit parade of examples. When it comes to the misuse of suffixes, what they seem to agree on hating most of all is the use of *hopefully* to mean, roughly, 'it is to be hoped that', or—as none of them would say—*fingers crossed*. In grammatical terms, they object to the use of *hopefully* as a 'sentence adverb', modifying a whole clause, rather than as an 'adverb of manner', modifying just a verb: they want 'Hopefully Bob checked the oven' to mean that Bob, in a state of hope, looked to see what was in the oven—not to express the speaker's hope that Bob ensured the meal would not burn. It might seem daft the extent to which use of *hopefully* in the latter sense bothers the gripers, given the abundance of parallel uses they merrily ignore (*clearly, obviously, surely*). Yet even the one they single out for special loathing can defeat them. Simon Heffer condemns the 'it-is-to-be-hoped' sense of *hopefully* as a 'peculiarly horrific popular use'. In his *Telegraph Style Guide*, 2010, however, he has failed to bother to edit the following introductory sentence: 'A newspaper develops a "house style" that is recognisable and, hopefully, in tune with its readership'. Kingsley Amis declares that those who use *hopefully* in this vague but coercive manner reveal themselves to be 'dimwits', and goes out on a limb in also disparaging the use of *thankfully* to mean, essentially, 'thank goodness'. But these objections already sound like a last hurrah, with the 'dimwits' interpreting the suffix *-fully* as they please.

And anyway, *hopefully* is the least of it. One wonders how the gripers shield themselves from the numerous other uses of affixes that ought also—surely—to distress them. Mercifully (some of them might say), the *OED* does not yet recognise *impactful*, *improvemental* or *cruxive*. But real life, in its mailshots and advertising copy, among its option traders and talking heads, does: 'Download the Impactful Marketing Manifesto'; 'Self improvemental posters for sale'; 'that's another cruxive circumstance'. And the *Guardian* is happy to give its readers this offering too: 'sullied by some innuendous stuff'. Whenever you spot such words shivering outside the dictionary—*brainsickly* dreamt up and *cannibally* put together—you could do worse, in your assault on Good English, than to try to help them find a way in.

14

ABSTRACT NOUNS

operationalisation

Now that we have had a look at affixes in general, let us consider a use of suffixes that yields example after example of a type of noun that the regulation griper abhors. Some of the horrible words we have so far encountered in this book could be characterised as good words out of place, just as a wildflower from the hedgerows found growing on a roundabout may be taken by council workers for a weed. But other sorts of horrible word are deemed by the gripers to be bad in and of themselves— irredeemably bad. And it is words of this second kind that will concern us here.

Percival Leigh, in his *Comic English Grammar* of 1840, mocks the idea—which he credits to Lindley Murray*—that a noun or 'substantive' should be defined metaphysically, for instance as 'the name of anything that exists, or of which we have any notion'. Leigh quotes a jokey piece of logic to show why this is a problem: 'A substantive is something, / But nothing is a substantive; / Therefore, nothing is something'. More seriously, he adds that 'A substantive may generally be known by its taking an article before it, and by its making sense of itself: as, a *treat*, the

---

* Lindley Murray was a highly prescriptive, hugely popular grammarian who began writing on the English language in the late eighteenth century. His work is treasured by the character Mrs Garth in *Middlemarch*.

mulligrubs, an *ache*'. Today's foremost linguists can also be found arguing that we go about matters backwards when we try to define a noun as a sort of 'thing': instead, they say, a noun is best understood as being any word that has the grammatical properties of a noun, and let 'thingness' take care of itself.* Yet this admirably graspable approach is not so helpful when what interests you is the concept of an 'abstract' noun, of which the word *thingness* would itself qualify as an example. And English speakers have somehow been managing to write about 'abstract nouns' for over six hundred years. There is, it is true, a grey area around this cat-egory. When Thomas Hardy's character Jude looks at Sue and sees the 'applelike convexities of her bodice, so different from Arabella's amplitudes', just how abstract *are* those convexities and amplitudes? One might conclude: not altogether. But even if the 'abstract noun' is a mere 'notion' whose margins are open to being queried, that does not stop the griper furiously resisting many new—or seemingly new—examples of this class of word. We too, therefore, shall cling to this label as having its uses.

Flick through any edition of the eighteenth-century dictionary of Nathan Bailey,[†] and you will find, before you even get past 'A', numerous forgotten abstract nouns. Some of them will be lost names for surviving entities: *abaction*, defined as the stealing of cattle, what we now call 'rustling'; *abligurition*, 'a prodigal spend-ing in Belly-Cheer': you know it when you see it. Others will be outré by comparison, 'things' defined by Bailey that no longer obviously need a name, e.g. *aestuary*, 'estuary', which he explains as meaning the 'receiving of Vapours or Steams of boiled Drugs in the Body, through a Hole made in a Seat or Chair'. As well as

---

* See for instance the writings on English grammar of Rodney Huddleston and Geoffrey K. Pullum.
† His *Universal Etymological English Dictionary*, which ran to numerous editions, was first published in 1721.

these, there will also be in a historical work such as Bailey's numerous variant forms of words that we continue to use, naming what
we still know as standard 'things'. Take the currently useful word
a *concern*: Bailey also supplies a 'concernment'. The *OED* dates
a *concern* back to 1589, then mentions that a *concerning*, dating to
1594, and sometimes used by Shakespeare, also meant a 'concern'.
It believes a *concernancy*, of 1604, a word apparently actually
invented by Shakespeare, possibly meant a 'concernment', but is
certain that a *concernance*, of 1645, meant a 'concernment'. So what
does the *OED* understand by a 'concernment'? This word, dating
from 1621, is defined by the *OED* as a 'concern'. Mildly foxing
this may be; however, the point of interest to us here is that for
a person wishing to conjure up new abstract nouns, there is an
oversupply of suffixes that will do the job.

Of course, an abstract noun does not always require a suffix,
as witness an *idea*, a *loss*, the *mulligrubs*. But plenty of the suffixes
that generate abstract nouns allow for the super-easy coining of
new examples.* The suffix *-ness* is incredibly handy. Add it to *red*
and you get *redness*, to *thing*, and you get *thingness*. Back around
1200, the word *skillwiseness* meant intelligence or reason; and
centuries later, *-ness* is still being pressed into widespread service,
as here: 'Speaking my mother tongue with my parents on an
everyday basis only cemented its kitchenness'; '. . . testament to
his wife's saintliness and his own pussy-whippedness'.† The same
sort of job is done by *-ity*: 'anyone who hopes to achieve virality
of any kind needs to think about how their message will work
on mobile' (*Guardian*); 'bejewelled with streams of ornament,

---

* A suffix that lends itself to being used in this way (as opposed to those
suffixes now out of use) is described by linguists as being 'productive'.
† See K. M. Hartmann, *Windows on the Abyss*, 2013, p. 149; and Antonya
Nelson, *Some Fun*, 2006, p. 34.

and shot through with a keening expressivity' (*Telegraph*); 'a Birtwistlean thrill ride of explosivity and stasis' (*Guardian*).

The construction *pussy-whippedness* may seem comical, from some points of view. And indeed, the ability to create novel, abstract 'thingnesses' has attracted many word-spinners of a humorous bent. Trawling the *OED*, we find some writers taking this to an extreme. George Sala, friend of Dickens, wrote in 1859 of an 'irreproachable state of clean-shirtedness, navy blue-broadclothedness and chimney-pot-hattedness'. Using an equally popular suffix, Horace Walpole, in 1784, playing on the idea of an 'airgonaut', coined *airgonation* to mean 'travelling by hot-air balloon'. Fanny Burney once described herself as suffering 'infinite *frettation*', while George Eliot, using yet another suffix, and in a more acerbic frame of mind, had Lydgate in *Middlemarch* decry London medical expertise as 'empty bigwiggism'. So useful is -*ism* in the language that it has long been discussed as a thing in itself. In 1809, the poet Robert Southey could write the impatient sentence, 'It has nothing to do with Calvinism nor Arminianism, nor any of the other *isms*'. Two years later, Shelley wrote similarly of someone who professed 'no "-ism" but superbism and irrationalism'. And in a modern echo, the dilatory Ferris Bueller, in 1986, would declare, 'Isms in my opinion are not good. A person should not believe in an ism'. If -*isms* are not good, however, Walpole and Burney's choice, an -*ation*, is, to a griper, even worse.

In one of his early plays, *Love's Labour's Lost*, Shakespeare created a pedant whom he mocked for being ludicrously fond of abstractions. Holofernes believes himself to have the gift of a spirit full of 'apprehensions, motions, revolutions'. In full flow, he manages to say, 'Most barbarous intimation! Yet a kind of insinuation, as it were, *in via*, of explication; *facere*, as it were, replication . . .'. Barbarous this may itself have been—but at least here Holofernes was sprinkling the suffix about. How much worse might it be to take two such words and use one to modify the other? No griper could applaud the phrase *devolution revolution*, applied repeatedly by our current governing classes not only to Scottish independence, but also to local council funding; could read cheerfully about 'consultation responses' to a proposed *information revolution* in the NHS; could sit still during a sermon on right speech given in Connecticut in 2012 under the title 'Disambiguation of Cogitation Situation'.*

But that is only the start. It is also a popular trick to slap *-ation* on the back end of a second suffix, say *-ize*. We have seen already that Ben Jonson raised an eyebrow back in 1631 when he introduced *problematise* into the English language. This word did not immediately flourish, and in John Craig's *New Universal Etymological, Technological, and Pronouncing Dictionary* of 1849, it is followed by the blunt note 'Not used'. There must be those who are sorry that John Craig was wrong about this. They will be even sorrier that *problematise* has since yielded *problematisation*.

Dickens takes a cool look at 'ization' in his novel of 1865, *Our Mutual Friend*. In it, Mr Podsnap, a smug, insular bully, is provoked by the poor taste of a 'meek man' who dares to mention in polite company that six or so people have recently starved to death on the streets of London. Podsnap declines to believe it. The meek man mentions the existence of inquest reports. Podsnap blames the victims. The meek man doubts that the victims wished to starve to death. Podsnap declares that no other country looks after its poor so well. The meek man suggests that that is all the more reason to find out what went wrong. Podsnap triumphantly remarks, 'I see what you are driving at. I knew it from the first. Centralization. No. Never with my consent. Not English'.

---

* Lincoln's dramatic blow against legal slavery in January 1863, for ever after known as the 'Emancipation Proclamation', was not actually issued under this title.

The meek man here submits that he was not aware of 'driving at any ization', and says that he is more staggered by the terrible deaths than by names 'of howsoever so many syllables'.

Podsnap's contempt for 'Centralization' is a blatant dodge: he floats the term in order to deride it. But the meek man—so rudely fobbed off—is himself no more enamoured of the banked-up suffixes. The two might even agree that a hint of fakery often clings to a word formed this way. The Bishop of Llandaff had written in 1836, 'all is "centralization," as it is called; a word not more strange to our language, than the practice, which it indicates, is foreign to our ancient habits and feelings'.* And a modern griper must also wonder drearily why a word like *premiumisation* ever had to be invented (so that readers of the *Telegraph* can learn about 'the continued premiumisation of sportswear'), let alone *otherisation*—to which comes the ready answer that 'it is often only by seeing things strangely that ideology and otherisation can be detected'.†

Perhaps even now you are noting to yourself that *centralisation* actually has three suffixes, the -*al* in the middle having been used to turn the noun *centre* into an adjective. Absolutely; and we now have *regionalisation* as well. But what do you get if you take that -*al* and stick it on one of our abstract nouns of the -*ation* kind? By this means, *inspiration* becomes *inspirational* (and leaves poor old *inspiring* in the dust), *transaction* becomes *transactional*, and *manipulation, manipulational,* as in: 'We refer here to the negative motivation regarding laboratory manipulational experiments . . .'. *Ablution* gives *ablutional,* which falls outside the notice of the *OED* but was used by Henry James when he referred to bathwater as 'ablutional fluid'; and *irritation* gives *irritational,* as used in a

* *A Charge delivered to the Clergy of the Diocese of Llandaff,* p. 33.
† Adrian Holliday, in *Issues in English Teaching,* Davison and Moss (eds.), 2000, p. 134.

report on a 'test for evaluation of irritational potential of dental materials'.*

The gripers will already be clutching their stomachs, but this is just the start. Take an adjective on these lines, and you can easily turn it into a new abstract noun, as *dimension* becomes *dimensional* becomes—in the hands of certain writers—*dimensionality*: Will Self, writing on the suburbs of Paris, remarks, 'But within this framing, content and dimensionality are provided by recent history'.† Better yet, take, oh, *operation*, make that into an adjective, *operational*, and then, remembering 'ize-mania' from Chapter 4, make that into a verb: *operationalise*—and then make *that* into another abstract noun, *operationalisation*, as here: 'Governmentalities are not just "govern mentalities"; they also refer to the operationalisation of knowledge . . .'. As ever, there are words on this pattern—with this pile-up of suffixes—that gripers will use quite happily, not one of them spitting their teeth out over, say, *rationalisation* (*ratio* shares its root with the word *reason*). Note, however, that even this word can be pushed beyond what a griper will tolerate by turning it back into an adjective: '. . . the meaningful associations were decisional rather than rationalizational' (we now have two -*tion*s and two -*al*s). Meanwhile, if *operationalisation* means something, can *operationalisational* be made to mean something too? Lo: 'Reassurance policing was tested as an operationalizational concept through the Home Office's National Reassurance Policing Programme'; '. . . operationalizational difficulties are so relevant', etc.‡

---

* See William J. McGuire, in *Interdisciplinary Relationships in the Social Sciences*, Sherif and Sherif (eds.), 2009, p. 31; Henry James's 1909 introduction to *The Golden Bowl*; and M. S. Koudi and Sanjayagouda B. Patil, *Prep Manual for Undergraduates: Dental Materials*, 2007, p. 22.
† *Guardian*, 14 November 2013.
‡ See Stephen Legg, *Spaces of Colonialism: Delhi's Urban Governmentalities*, 2007, p. 11; Carter and Wilkins (eds.), *Probation and Parole: Selected Readings*,

You may be thinking that in your enormous efforts to impinge slightly on the limits set around Good English, you might just pass over the matter of abusing abstract nouns, not least because there appear to be so many people in on this game already. But why not embrace the 'normalisational aspects' of joining in?* In the spirit of superbism,† simply take a suffix or two—or three, or four, or five—and give way to your Frankenstein instincts! Run the galvanic power of noun-ness through the dead frog of the abstract or even doubly abstract 'thing' you are trying to create—throw in perhaps a couple of adjectival jolts for good measure, and a dose of verbifying too. The gripers, seeing your efforts towards the *operationalisation* of one of these sparky monsters, must cry, 'That is not a living word!' It will be your job, in defying them, to attempt to keep the wretched creature going.

1970, p. 347; Rob C. Mawby, in *Dictionary of Policing*, Newburn and Neyroud (eds.), 2013, p. 237; and Sandro Castaldo, *Trust in Market Relationships*, 2007, p. 215.

* '. . . this comparison enables a focus on the normalisational aspects of this condition': Renos K. Papadopoulos and Judy Hildebrand, in *Multiple Voices: Narrative in Systemic Family Psychotherapy*, Papadopoulos and Byng-Hall (eds.), 1997, p. 207.

† NB Arthur Koestler coined the excellent term *wasm* to denote an ex-ism (see *Promise and Fulfilment*, 1949, p. 54).

15

NEGATIVES; OPPOSITES

disinterested, outro

In the opening statement of *Paradise Lost*, Milton chooses to emphasise, not wrong, so much as failure-to-do-right: his great work will speak, 'Of man's first disobedience ...'. And Walter Chalmers Smith, in his hymnal of 1867, similarly opts to use several opposites, or 'antonyms', in an attempt to approach the subject of divinity: 'Immortal, invisible, God only wise, / In light inaccessible hid from our eyes ...'. In both cases, implicit comparisons—with being obedient, mortal, visible, accessible—are generated through the use of negative prefixes, here *dis-*, *im-* and *in-*.*

There are other rhetorical effects to be wrung from negatives. They can, for instance, be comic. Shakespeare treads a risky line with the humour of Sonnet 130. He starts, 'My mistress' eyes are nothing like the sun; / Coral is far more red than her lips' red', and then continues with many further comparisons in the same vein. It is therefore something of a relief to the reader when he ends: 'And yet, by heaven, I think my love as rare / As any she belied with false compare'. In his 1823 revision of Francis Grose's *Classical Dictionary of the Vulgar Tongue*, Pierce Egan details a less

---

* When it comes to adding negative affixes to words, it is, for reasons not entirely obvious, prefixes that dominate. (And this is true even if you choose to weigh the contraction *-n't* in the balance.)

high-flown example of calculated reversal. The word *bender*, he says, is 'ironical': 'if one asks another to do any act which the latter considers unreasonable or impracticable, he replies, O, yes, I'll do it—Bender; meaning, by the addition of the last word, that, in fact, he will do no such thing'. A couple of centuries later, the same trick would be used, to serenely puerile effect, in the film *Wayne's World*, the delayed terminal interjection in this case being *not*. Though the consequent fad for the last-minute *not* may have annoyed gripers at the time, this use of *not* was far from being new. Indeed, the *OED* traces it back through multiple examples to George Eliot's *Mill on the Floss*: 'Did she feel as he did? He hoped she did—not'.

If one were to give this subject next to no thought at all, it might seem fair to assume that, just as *bender* was once used to turn a statement into its own opposite, so our negative prefixes—*dis-*, *im-*, *in-*, *non-*, *de-*, *un-*, *ig-*, *ab-*, and more—exist simply in order that an amenable word can be made to mean its own reverse: thus *dis-* makes *disagreeable* from *agreeable*, *de-* and *un-* make *defreeze* and *unfreeze* from *freeze*, and so on. Put another way, though it might now be hard to work out why *unashamed* came into the language in 1600, or *unserious* a few decades later, when these words were wanted, they were easy enough to create.

But as ever with English, a straightforward picture is more than likely to be misleading. For a start, and odd as this may at first appear, negative constructions are perfectly capable of changing meaning over time. The words *invaluable* and *priceless*, sixteenth-century coinages, both now mean, broadly, 'of incalculable worth'. Yet both for spells in their histories were also used to mean 'of no worth at all', which is to say 'worthless'.* Again,

---

* There are many sentences where the words *invaluable* and *priceless* would be interchangeable, though by convention, a hilarious joke is in some dialects 'priceless' but not 'invaluable'; wonderful advice, 'invaluable' but not 'priceless'.

disbelief, in the past, meant, as the *OED* explains, 'positive unbelief', so that the character in George Eliot's novel *Daniel Deronda* who feels a 'new disbelief in the worth of men' has lost belief in the worth of men. Now, however, *disbelief* can be used to suggest something much more like 'resistance in the face of stunned amazement that X should be true', as in, 'I stared in disbelief at my measly bank balance'. In related fashion, we have lost the early sense of *discover*—more or less conveyed, now, by *disclose* or *uncover*—as is clear when Addison, in a *Spectator* essay of 27 June 1711, provides remarks on the flirtatious opening of a fan: an act delightful 'as it discovers on a sudden an infinite Number of *Cupids*, Garlands, Altars, Birds, Beasts, Rainbows, and the like agreeable Figures'. The word *disappoint* has strayed even further from its original meaning. Because it really did once suggest 'dis-appoint', or as we might now say *unseat*, *dispossess* or even, in today's language, *sack* (or *rationalise* or *adjust*), it is not wholly strange that we have come to use it for variations on *baulk*, *foil* and *let down*. But its modern meaning (whose usefulness may be judged from the number of words required to explain it properly) is far from being the opposite of *appoint* or 'prefer for office'. The opposite of *inhibit* used to be *exhibit* but is now *disinhibit*; the opposite of the noun *ease* used to be *disease* but is now *unease*, *discomfort*—and so on.*

---

* There are various words in English that many people wrongly understand to begin with a negative prefix, causing them some puzzlement. If one must *unpick* the stitches of a too-tight garment, how is it that to 'pick' stitches has never meant to sew them? (It used to be possible to 'unpick' a lock as well.) Why are *spoil* and *despoil* not opposites, and why do *thaw* and *unthaw* mean the same thing? More obscurely, how is it that the fifteenth-century word *notwithstanding* means 'despite' when *notagainstanding*, another word from the same period (in which *again* is a shortened form of *against*), also meant 'despite'? And why is it—in a widely celebrated example—that *flammable* and *inflammable* both mean 'flammable'? The answer to this one is that the prefix *in-* is not here a negative, but is used in the sense of 'bringing into a certain

Some of our negatives have, over the course of centuries, lost their positives. The adjectives *exorable* and *consolate* each lasted about three hundred years, then died. *Unruly*, dating from around 1400, was once matched by *ruly*—but *ruly* faded out again. *Wieldy*, which originally meant 'nimble', is now extremely rare. And we can *disparage*, but the word *parage*, meaning 'rank', is long gone. Some negatives, moreover, have never had a positive at all. The word *disastrous* is formed from parts meaning, essentially, 'ill-starred', but there has never been an *astrous* in the language to mean 'fortunate'; nor has *indignant* ever been twinned with *dignant*, which by its etymology would mean something like 'reverential'. With a stranded negative, there can arise the temptation to deploy its technical opposite, sometimes labelled a 'pseudo-antonym', especially when the result sounds comical: *combobulated*, *gormful*, *ert*,* and so on. The word *trepidatious*, as the opposite of *intrepid*, apparently dreamt up by Bertram Mitford in 1904, is still inching its way into the language a century later—much though some gripers find it wanting. R. H. Fiske, it is no surprise to discover, writes that 'except among those who flout understanding' *trepidatious* is 'not a word'.

Of course, opposites or notional opposites are not always formed using negatives. In a particularly daft example, our old friend Thomas Nashe, in 1589, coined the idea of going on *footback* as the wonky alternative to *horseback*. And no less wonky-seeming is the concept of the *downcrease* now creeping into the outer

---

state', just as *insure* means, by its etymology, 'make safe'. The prefix *with-* in *withstand* actually has the sense 'against', a meaning repeated in a few other extremely old words, such as *wipsprecan*, 'withspeak', which meant 'contradict'. The *de-* in *despoil* emphasises thoroughness, as it does also in, for instance, *denude*. And the *un-* in *unpick* and *unthaw*, as well as in *unpeel*, *unloose*, and others, is classed by the *OED* as simply redundant (and by ill-informed gripers—at least in *unthaw*—as illogical and incorrect).

* The *ert* in *inert* (and in *inertia*) is, in fact, related to the word *art*.

reaches of unsifted English: 'The critical form of anthropology . . . is a much more recent development and ironically is on the down-crease'. Also wonky, in its own way, is the word *old-fangled*. This adjective has lurked about in the language for a couple of centuries or more, and today has special currency among sellers of weatherproof ceramic fairies and horoscope tea towels, who use it as a dewy substitute for *old-fashioned*. Not that it makes any difference, but the history of the word, though opaque, is against this. After entering English in the fourteenth century, *newfangle*—later *newfangled*—came to be used to describe both what was trivially or disquietingly new, and the state of mind of a person weak enough to be seduced by such novelties. (Marvell, in 1670, wrote of 'All the French curiosityes and trinkets, of which our people are so new-fangled'.) Given that this suspect, light-weight side to *newfangled* has persisted in modern usage, *old-fangled*, interpreted as its direct opposite, ought perhaps to suggest, not 'old-fashioned', but something more illogical like 'old-vamped', or even 'old-trinketed', or, as a modern interior decorator might say, 'artfully distressed'—but when did logic ever hold sway in these matters? The two earliest known uses of *old-fangled* come from the novel *Triumvirate* of 1764, written, it so happens, by Richard Griffith (see pp. 31 and 95), who plainly saw the word as amusing: 'I was really, as much puzzled, as old Square Toes, himself, to know how to deal with her old-fangled notions, as he stiled them'. There is also an example of its use in Robert Browning's 1842 poem 'The Pied Piper of Hamelin', when Browning notes the Piper's 'quaint' attire and hanging pipe: 'low it dangled / Over his vesture so old-fangled'. If this was not simply illiterate, then Browning must have wished to invoke, by paradox, 'shoddy gaudiness'. Shakespeare, it has to be said, in Sonnet 91, managed to sidestep all this bother by speaking of garments 'new-fangled ill'.

In the case of *old-fangled*, the meaning of what on the face of it is an opposite has been arrived at by wayward custom; and as we have seen, it is also often custom, not logic, that governs the meaning of opposites formed by adding a negative prefix. In *The Cloud of Unknowing*, a superlative work of medieval mysticism, the experience of 'unknowyng' is presented as something sublimely other than the base state of 'ignoraunce', yet on etymology alone, the meaning of these two words should be identical.* And having rival opposites in the language is perfectly normal too: *moral* gives rise to *immoral* and *amoral*; *lawful*, to *unlawful* and *lawless*; *qualified*, to *unqualified* and *disqualified*; *information*, to *misinformation* and *disinformation*; *use*, to *misuse*, *disuse* and *abuse*—and so on.

But what happens when the meanings of these words become a matter of dispute? No griper today calls it 'abominable' when *disbelief* is used to mean 'amazement'; or *disappointed*, to mean 'let down'; or *disease*, to mean 'sickness'; or *discover*, to mean 'find out'. But there is one word where a popular interpretation of the prefix *dis-* makes them half furious, half miserable. We have met it already, more than once.[†] Kingsley Amis described it as 'The most famous and ancient of all misuses and not for that reason any less a case of ignorant bullshit', classing the word itself as a 'depraved form'. With equal heat, but drawing a different conclusion, Simon Heffer applies the term 'abuser' to anyone who gives it what he considers the wrong sense. Mr Fiske not only agrees with this, but is so exercised by the supposed misuse at issue that he calls it 'a diminution of the foremost way in which we maintain our humanity: using language effectively'.

---

* Ask a lawyer the difference between 'not guilty' and 'innocent', and you will want to settle yourself in a comfortable chair for the answer—though for a reasonably snappy explanation, see Bryan A. Garner, *Garner's Modern American Usage*, 2003, p. 555.
† See especially p. 79.

The word is *disinterested*. Mr Heffer condemns out of hand those who use it to mean 'uninterested' (finding something uninteresting) rather than 'impartial' (having no interest or stake in a matter). *The Economist Style Guide* agrees: '*disinterested* means *impartial*; *uninterested* means *bored*'. John Humphrys, in *Lost for Words*, declares that *disinterested* means something different from *uninterested* 'and that's that': anyone who believes otherwise has 'got it wrong'. The *OED*, meanwhile, merrily supplies examples right the way back to the early 1600s both of *disinterested* being used to mean 'unconcerned'—not least in the work of John Donne—and of *uninterested* being used to mean 'impartial'—not least in the work of Byron. This is the reverse of the diktat of today's gripers, and the matter has never been as clear in practice as those who currently rule on it might wish. So the anger rumbles on.

The battle over *disinterested* has been waged for decades now, but there are other, more recent opposites that also get the grumblers going. Even where a new opposite is formed in a fully sanitary manner, it is in danger of attracting dislike simply because it *is* new. A century ago *demote*, as the novel opposite of the age-old *promote*, had to struggle for acceptance: 'When absentees returned to school, the masters were unwilling to "demote" them' (*Daily News*, 1900). No one would put *demote* in inverted commas now. But the more recent coinage *exfiltrate*, CIA slang for smuggling recaptured hostages out of enemy territory, and impeccably the opposite of *infiltrate*, will probably sound funny to those who have never heard it before. A word also impeccably formed, *prepone*, though it may also sound peculiar to many, was used in the sixteenth century to mean 'set before', and is now used, mostly in Indian English, to mean 'bring forward'—Bollywood gossip reveals that 'the release of *Shuddh Desi Romance* has been preponed'. And among computer programmers, *prepend* as the opposite of *append* is noticeably on the rise. The 1960s coinage *disbenefit* will sound off-kilter to some, unlike *disadvantage*, one assumes—but this is perhaps in part because of the contexts in which *disbenefit* gets used. For instance, the mealy-mouthed strapline 'Understanding the Disbenefit if Respite is Encroached Upon' comes in a report on the threat of greater noise at Heathrow Airport.

Where the unimpeachably assembled *disbenefit* and *prepone* still perhaps sound awkward, the mangled coinage *prequel* is now widely accepted, presumably because it is so useful. However, there may be disquiet for some time to come at increasing use of *outro* to mean the concluding part of a piece of music or of a show. In 1935, A. P. Herbert railed against *television* as 'a monster—half Greek, half Latin': he reckoned that, for purity's sake, the device should have been called a 'teleopsis'. One can only imagine that *outro* would have made him rail the more. It splits the Latin *intro-* in two, then replaces *in* with the Germanic *out*, making *outro* not merely an impure monster, but a poor butchered monster of a word. The obvious alternative would be *extro*; yet *outro* is proving serviceable, so does any of this really matter?

It should by now seem completely inconsequential that the Americans have developed the ability to say 'I could care less' to convey the meaning 'I couldn't care less'; but only declare yourself *disinterested*, and perhaps *underwhelmed* while you are at it, and you too will be away. It is hardly a *brainer** that new negatives and opposites will cause the gripers at large to fuss; indeed, as we now know, if you join the shock troops in this corner of the language, you will cause the more excessive of the huffers and

* 'Me? Very much a brainer': Debbie Johnson, *Dark Vision*, 2014, p. 302; 'It's a brainer. It's a total brainer': Scott Kelby, *Scott Kelby's Digital Photography Boxed Set*, 2014, p. 23.

puffers to detect a 'diminution of your humanity'. Let them, and try not to *pregret** in the process the contempt your work will bring down on your head. If your campaign is ever to succeed, you must *underbear*† the counter-attacks to come.

* '*Pregret* was more like it': Jennifer Weiner, *Then Came You*, 2011, p. 130.
† Why the English would let slip a word for suffering, it is hard to imagine. *Underbear* is found in the language from around 950, and stayed in use for several centuries afterwards.

16

DOUBLE NEGATIVES

irregardless

You may have been wondering why you should concern yourself with the effects of single negatives when you could so easily pile in with several. And it is true that the 'double negative', in particular, has its own potential to cause annoyance—as can be deduced from the heat with which this construction is condemned by our advisers. Simon Heffer, for example, roundly denounces double negatives as 'offences against logic', and says that they have 'no place in civilised writing'. But why? Committed pedants rule that two negatives cancel each other out.* And simply as a matter of good style, Mr Heffer believes, one should express one's thoughts in a positive form. 'Why write "no-one is missing"', he asks, 'when one means "everyone is here"?'

The Greeks gave the name 'litotes' to the rhetorical figure explained by the *OED* as that 'in which an affirmative is expressed by the negative of the contrary'.† Mr Heffer's analysis implies that use of litotes is somehow a sign of limp thinking. But if it strikes

---

* There is a famous story of an exchange on this point between the philosophers J. L. Austin and Sidney Morgenbesser. James Ryerson's obituary for Morgenbesser in the *New York Times Magazine*, 26 December 2004, describes how Austin, during a lecture, explained that a double negative gives a positive, but 'never does a double positive amount to a negative', causing Morgenbesser to mutter loudly, 'Yeah, yeah'.
† Litotes is *not uncommonly* achieved through the use of two negatives, but it is

you that this is to sell nuance short, then you are not far wrong. One would feel concerned for him if, faced with a pair of valentines, one saying, 'I love you', and the other, 'I don't not love you', he could really draw no greater distinction between them than that the first was neatly expressed, and the second, not. Even Lindley Murray saw more flexibility in the figure than this, writing that double negatives allow for 'a pleasing and delicate variety of expression'.*

Just in case his readers remain unpersuaded, Mr Heffer further rules on double negatives that they are 'unfunny if they attempt to be humorous, arch if they attempt to be anything else', and again, that if they 'are an attempt at being funny, they fail'. By these bluff standards, Addison, who in his notes on *Paradise Lost* [†] was not attempting to be funny, must have been being arch (not to mention uncivilised) when he observed that Milton, to avoid shocking his readers with Satan's impieties, took care to introduce 'none that is not big with absurdity'. Mr Heffer would require this to be rewritten as 'only those that are big with absurdity'. But Addison was keen to accentuate the negative—as why not?— and to make Milton's choice here more explicitly an act of exclusion. Archness had nothing to do with it.

Meanwhile, thank goodness nobody persuaded Laurence Sterne to believe that where double negatives are an 'attempt' at being funny, 'they fail'. In a meandering tale in *Tristram Shandy*

---

no challenge to find examples of the figure that use only one. The affirmative arrived at in this manner is not always wholly explicit (*not half*).

* Just occasionally one meets a use of a double negative that really might give a reader pause, as in the sentence 'Few doubt that certain views pervade and practices persist but even fewer will own up to holding them or following them' (*Guardian*). Here, the negative expression 'few doubt' conveys the positive sense 'many believe', so that the reader who has mentally established those 'many' as the subject will then trip over 'even fewer . . .'.

[†] *The Spectator*, 16 February 1712.

about a parson lending his horse to all comers, we have it explained to us that this fellow 'was not an unkind-hearted man'. This amusingly cheese-paring form of words turns into a joke of a more disturbing kind when it hits home that, by this expression, the wrong negative quality is being disavowed. The parson, imposed upon on all sides, has generously but weakly lent out his horse so often that it has been ruined by others. He might have been not-unkind-hearted in his relations with those unscrupulous folk whom he helped, but that is not to say that he was unequivocally 'kind-hearted': think of the poor horse.

Though Addison's 'none that is not big' is rhetorically distinct from 'only those that are big', on bald logic alone, the two phrases lead to the same practical result: either way round, the same absurd examples of Satan's impieties end up being included in *Paradise Lost*. There is, however, a use of multiple negatives that defies this stolid analysis. Louis Armstrong gives a beautiful demonstration in his remark that 'the music ain't worth nothing if you can't lay it on the public'.* With litotes, the maths holds up (for instance, 'not nothing' would be used to imply 'something'). But the repeated negatives of Armstrong's sentence are being used for emphasis (the music is worth absolutely *nothing* if no audience gets to hear it), making this an example of what linguists call 'negative concord'.

Mr Heffer remarks that deploying negatives for emphasis in this way 'is a common feature of vulgar usage'. Confident of his ground, he adds, 'such forms can safely be regarded as already outside the lexicon of those aiming to write correct English, so we need not trouble ourselves further with them'. Perhaps he should have thought a little harder about the vulgar side of his remark. Lindley Murray supplies the following example of

* See Joshua Berrett, *The Louis Armstrong Companion*, 1999, p. xiv.

negative concord: 'I never did repent of doing good, nor shall not now'. Is this outside Mr Heffer's lexicon? (Murray proposes that the 'not' should be replaced with *I*.) W. E. Henley, meanwhile, author of the poem *Invictus*—master of his fate, captain of his soul, and the model, after he had a leg removed, for Long John Silver—cheerfully wrote in 1884 in a letter to Robert Louis Stevenson, 'I shouldn't wonder if we don't continue to do a miracle, & pay our expenses'. But perhaps that really *was* a vulgar thing to say. Back in 1939, in *Good and Bad English*, Whitten and Whitaker noted, as all who consider this topic must, that even Shakespeare used negative concord in his writing once in a while: 'Nor what he spake, though it lacked form a little, / Was not like madness' (*Hamlet*); 'Nor let no comforter delight mine ear' (*Much Ado about Nothing*). But their comment on this was that although 'the meaning is clear enough',* still, 'the illogicality is no longer pardoned'. Pardoned by whom, one dares to wonder, and in what circumstances, then or now? Our late Prime Minister, for one, might like to be forgiving. Never mind his education at Eton and Oxford; his distant cousinship of the Queen: on *Today*, Radio 4, 18 January 2015, he rued a finding that in Britain 'there are 38,000 Muslim women who really don't hardly speak any English at all'.

Examples of litotes and negative concord can also be found packed into single words. Shakespeare was sufficiently intrigued by the drama of negative reverses that he decided to coin his own one-word double negative, dropping it into a high-stakes logical argument in *The Comedy of Errors*. Adriana, addressing her supposed husband (actually, his identical twin), tries to persuade him out of what appears to be infidelity. First she says that if she were

---

* The meaning with negative concord is indeed almost always completely clear. Faced by a person growling, 'I don't owe you no money', would even Mr Heffer reply, 'Oh, marvellous: if it's all the same to you, I'll take it now, thanks'?

stained by her own act of infidelity, he would hate it. Then she says that, as they are one in marriage, even if it is he who is unfaithful, she is no less contaminated by his act. It follows, she argues, that he ought to find her contamination by *this* means equally—prohibitively—hateful and shameful:

> For if we two be one, and thou play false,
> I doe digest the poison of thy flesh,
> Being strumpeted by thy contagion:
> Keepe then faire league and truce with thy true bed,
> I live distain'd,* thou undishonoured.

Shakespeare's idea of being *undishonoured* evidently struck a chord, as the word found a place in the writings of many who came after him. The same cannot be said for Jeremy Bentham's eye-watering invention, *undisfulfilled.†*

Undishonoured and even *undisfulfilled* were both litotical inventions. Of all the disparaged single-word double negatives, however, the reigning queen is *irregardless*, and this is no doubt in part because it more closely conforms to the mechanics of negative concord. People who loudly love Good English are disgusted by this word—if they even agree that it *is* one. Kingsley

---

* This is the wording used in the First Folio. Inconveniently, but perhaps not to the amazement of a reader of the previous chapter, the meaning of *distained* in Shakepeare's time appears to have been what we now mean by 'stained'. Editors of *The Comedy of Errors* have tried to get round the difficulty this seems to pose by altering the text to read 'unstain'd' or 'dis-stained'.
† It is not so hard to think of *un-dis* words in English, but most do not follow the double-negative pattern of *undishonoured*. For example, *undisguised* does not mean not-not-dressed, because to *disguise* has never been the opposite of to 'guise'; *discouraged*—giving *undiscouraged*—is not the opposite of 'couraged'; and *dismayed*—giving *undismayed*—is not the opposite of 'mayed'. The idea of the '*undismembered* Empire' had a brief life in English thought, and was used cuttingly by John Betjeman in his poem of 1940 'In Westminster Abbey' ('Gracious Lord, oh bomb the Germans'). But the word has now slunk back out of use.

Amis described *regardless* as having been 'blown up' into *irregardless* through a 'kind of illiteracy', with the negative prefix *ir-* added to *regardless* in half-baked tribute to *irrespective*. Even 'non-pedantic' Oliver Kamm baulks at it, writing that *regardless* 'will do the job precisely', and that *irregardless* is 'unnecessary' (as though that makes any difference). Logically, goes the desperate argument of the gripers, *ir-* and *-less* must cancel each other out, so that if *irregardless of* has to be used at all, it should at least be used to mean 'with regard for', instead of what it is actually used to mean—*regardless*—the word it simultaneously bastardises and threatens to replace.

Perhaps *irregardless* sounds to its detractors like a modern invention, typical of our dunderheaded times. It was used in 2006 to what may well have been eye-widening effect by the principal of a grammar school in a written statement submitted to a parliamentary select committee: 'girls who live at a distance from the school, irregardless of their educational needs, will inevitably be denied access to a grammar school education'. But is *irregardless* really so new? No. Among other early uses, the following remark was published in 1865: 'but our Surgeon, irregardless alike of either privilege or regulation . . .'.*

And as it happens, English has been here before. In his dictionary, Johnson called *irresistless* 'A barbarous ungrammatical conjunction of two negatives'. Again, the 'two negatives' business by itself is not automatically a problem: Johnson was happy to explain without nasty comments that *undisobliging* meant 'inoffensive'. The problem he had with *irresistless* was that it was being used to mean 'irresistible', and not (as logic might be thought to dictate) 'resistible', or 'irresistible—*bender*'. An eighteenth-century paraphrase of the *Song of Solomon* written by

* Frederick E. Cushman, *History of the 58th Regt. Massachusetts Vols. From the 15th day of September, 1863, to the Close of the Rebellion*, p. 18.

a forgotten Irish academic demonstrates the sort of use that was getting Johnson down. In a catastrophically bad poem, a line that is given by the Authorized Version of the Bible as 'Thou hast ravished my heart' becomes 'Love, irresistless, has possess'd / With all his Fires, my glowing Breast'.* Was this supposed to suggest 'love resistible'? No. But that, the Johnsonian gripe implied, was what it did in fact mean.

The *OED* supplies a single instance of the adverb *irrelentlessly*, used in 1624 by Richard Montagu, future Bishop of Norwich. *Irresistless*, from the 1650s on, had a much more successful run. You might like to consider it as a candidate for revival: this would surely cause the gripers acute despair. But if efforts in that direction seem to require too much of you, do at least think of deploying its depraved echo *irregardless*: this word may have more than a toehold in the language, but it still needs help to secure a firmer place. Superfluous negatives—superfluous according to our advisers—are found all over English usage. Who are the gripers to dictate what everyone else should mean by them? Be brave, stare down your *unforbidding*† foes, and one of your sallies will *undoubtlessly*‡ find its mark.

---

* Charles Johnson, *The Song of Solomon Paraphrased; in Lyrick Verse*, 1751, p. 14.
† 'The rugged, unforbidding wilderness of Badlands National Park' (*Guardian*); 'they jealously protect their own fiefs by demolishing our versions with unforbidding scorn': Ben Agger, *The Decline of Discourse: Reading, Writing and Resistance in Postmodern Capitalism*, 1990, p. 83. (The word *forbid* joins *for-*, a negative prefix, to *bid*, an Old English verb meaning 'offer'. The adjective *forbidding* has therefore traditionally meant 'off-putting' or 'uninviting'—as, evidently, *unforbidding* now does too.)
‡ 'Undoubtlessly, new dedicated tools and techniques will be developed': S. Kleinhans et al., in *Benchmarking—Theory and Practice*, Asbjørn Rolstadås (ed.), 2013, p. 276; '. . . the texturation process is undoubtlessly the most valuable way for obtaining high critical current density values . . .': R. Cloots et al., in *Supermaterials*, Cloots et al. (eds.), 2000, p. 153.

17

WORD INFLATION

precautious

Those critics who spurn negative concord insist on seeing snaggly illogic where the rest of the world sees nothing more pernicious than emphasis. Moving on from this, it should surprise no one to discover that in English there are other forms of emphasis—or what the naysayers will insist on thinking of as *overemphasis*—that provoke grief and finger-wagging. This brings us conveniently to a topic known to linguists as 'word inflation'.

There are various ways in which a bit of lexical oomph can be added to our regular vocabulary. The impulse to beef up a word by sticking on a prefix and interpreting it as an intensifier ('morphemic pleonasm') is one that inspires considerable scorn among those who care about such things. *The Economist Style Guide* remarks that '*Pre-prepared* just means *prepared*'—as others grumble that *preplanned* just means 'planned'. Brilliantly, *The Economist* also rules against *skyrocket* as being both 'unnecessarily long' and, worse, American. (It also dislikes *proactive*. This is 'Not a pretty word', it says, 'try *active*'.) In similar style, Bill Bryson dismisses *co-equal* as 'fatuous', before going on to suggest that the *pre-* of *precondition* 'should be deleted'. But if so—if *precondition* should be chopped down to size—what, you might wonder, of *predominate*? Is this word 'unnecessarily long'—try *dominate*? Should the front ends not also be deleted from *prerequisite* and *despoil*? And ought not the gripers to have been resisting *overwhelm* long before the world came up with *underwhelm* (the verb *whelm* without the *over* meaning 'overturn', so that *overwhelm* could be interpreted as meaning 'over-overturn', or, of all things, metaphorically, 'put to rights')? Before the 1930s, *twined* was more popular than *intertwined*. Which version of the word would the average griper reach for now? And what of *intermingle*? Is *intermingle* really more minglesome than *mingle* on its own? Your mind may have started to spin, but warned is armed: do not ask these questions of the gripers. If you try it, you will cause them to up the stakes further.

Flyweight huffers and puffers might stumble over an argument about *intermingle* or *despoil*, but the purest purist will immediately come back at you with the use of *epicentre* as a supercharged version of *centre*. *Epicentre*, this person will explain wearyingly, is drawn from the terminology of the earthquake and kindred phenomena, whose centre, main event or 'focus' occurs *under* a surface: 'epicentre' is the technical name for the point on the surface immediately *above* the focus. To any such explanation you must reply that enormous numbers of people find this distinction of absolutely no interest whatsoever, and that, like it or not, *epicentre* now also means the 'really really central centre'.* At this, the griper, teeth gritted, is likely to up the ante once again by pointing to the ignorant boosterism of using *penultimate* to mean, not 'the one before last', but something along the lines of 'super-ultimate'— as it does in the following generous comment, which describes a certain book as having 'gone deeply into the understanding of human behavior and what is really needed to enhance our personalities and achieve penultimate success'; or as it does in a work

* Granted, it was bold of the writer Erin Cressida Wilson to put an 'epicentre' underground: 'If the city and our house felt like extensions of all things carnal, then our derelict basement seemed to be the epicentre': *Guardian*, 27 November 2014.

discussing the idea that 'The penultimate or peak in the psycho-pathological process of the suicide bomber is the choice to activate the choice to die and kill'.* While you struggle with this, your griper will probably already be moving on to the word *precautious*. Sometimes it is used with reference to the taking of precautions; but it is also currently at risk of meaning 'very very cautious'—and either way, it is bound to be classed as vile. What, your sarcastic friend will ask, does Clarence Talley mean by his 'golden nugget of wisdom' that, 'With the poor still among us in this twenty-first century, we should be extra precautious about leftovers'?† What was Gertrude Stein on about, a hundred years earlier, when she wrote in 'Portrait of Prince B. D.': 'The change is not present and the sensible way to have agony is not precautious'?

Having replied to these challenges with no more than a mysterious smile, you may well be reflecting that every last part of the griper's tirade can be taken as evidence of the fact that from time to time we ('we' broadly speaking) like to give a word a bit of a lift. *Mania*, for example, was perfectly serviceable for about 450 years. Then all of a sudden: *megalomania*. In *Christian Work*, 1 February 1867, in an account of a thieving vicar, the then-new form of the word is offered up with a touch of disdain. The cleric's defence in court of insanity, 'or megalomania, as it was called', seems not to have been supported by any evidence other than that of the crime itself. Yet by 1900, the *megalomaniac* was everywhere. *Omnishambles*, a coinage of 2012, entered common parlance with even greater speed. Then again, though *omnishambles* may currently convey something more shambolic than a humble *shambles*, it is perfectly possible that before too long there will be little to

---

* See the back-jacket puff for Karan Sondhi, *Persona Magnified*, 2007; and Israel W. Charny, *Fighting Suicide Bombing*, 2007, p. 83.
† Dr Clarence Talley, Sr, *From the Pulpit to the Streets: Golden Nuggets of Wisdom for Daily Living*, 2012, p. 61.

choose between the naked word—if it even survives—and the accessorised version.

Dressing up a perfectly good word with a needless prefix, as the griper might see it, is easy enough. Even easier is to drag strong terms away from their literal or customary context so as to exploit the hyperbolic qualities they then impart elsewhere. But this effect can be short-lived. Poor *stratospheric* has been lowered, wretched *abysmal* has been raised and *cataclysmic*, 'in the manner of a mighty flood', now mops up after workaday exaggerations. In a *Telegraph* sports report, what is referred to first as a referee's 'high-profile error' becomes, later in the article, a 'cataclysmic cock-up': the person who clings to a traditional understanding of cataclysms will hardly know where to look.

The rhetorical value of restraint may appeal to some: 'here goes nothing', as computer gamers mutter when they are about to attempt an insanely difficult move. And with a formula of this kind, the currency should remain reasonably stable. But hyperbole is different. Adjectives especially—a *wicked*, an *epic*—are wont to crash on the sandbanks of emphasis, only to retreat with a melancholy, long, withdrawing roar. Nor is this a recent phenomenon. From around 1400, and for centuries afterwards, the word *unspeakable* was used to denote religious ineffability. But with the ascent of Queen Victoria to the throne, it was toppled, and became in particular an insult used by snobs who wished to dismiss this or that as indescribably unimpressive. Even now, a person reading in the Authorized Version of the Bible 'Thanks be unto God for his unspeakable gift' (2 Cor. ix. 15) may find it necessary to edit away the sudden picture of God as some ghastly parvenu who has given china wall-ducks as a wedding present.* *Awful*, which for centuries meant 'awe-inspiring', suffered the same fate as

* The New English Bible translates 'his unspeakable gift' as 'his gift beyond words'.

unspeakable, and at more or less the same time; by the 1940s, Ivor Brown, in *A Word in Your Ear*, was willing to declare that 'no word' had been 'more foully mishandled' (the downfall of *awesome* was yet to come). As for the use of *literally* to mean, not literally 'literally', but figuratively 'figuratively'—or not even that: its use merely as an intensifier—the ink wasted decrying this shift would be enough to make a squid despair.*

The dwindling of the rhetorical force (the 'semantic bleaching') of such words as *epic*, *abysmal* and *awesome* mirrors the fate of many stock phrases that use repetition for emphasis. A rush of negatives is by no means the only way that this is achieved. For starters, there are numerous standard pairs in English, the stagey *lo and behold*, the strategic *all well and good, but . . .*, the teasing *maybe, maybe not.*† Expressions of this kind can become so deeply embedded in the language that their duplicate nature rarely strikes us; and if it ever does, they probably still feel right and proper, and we happily pass on by. There are also single-word examples of this doubling. Consider *haphazard*. *Hazard* is a word of Arabic origin meaning 'chance'. *Hap*, as in *perhaps* or *happen*, originally Scandinavian, also means 'chance'. Thus one might argue that *haphazard* could as well be 'haphap' or 'hazardhazard'. The word *forefront* is, for complicated reasons, almost the same. In its earliest use, *fore* meant 'front' and *front* meant 'face'. The two were put together to allow for discussion of the 'front face' of a building—as opposed to its 'back face' or indeed its 'back front', or, in current

* On *literally*, Ambrose Bierce wrote in 1909, 'It is bad enough to exaggerate, but to affirm the truth of the exaggeration is intolerable'. Oliver Kamm, who tells his readers to 'embrace the language that you already speak and write', nevertheless condemns 'the non-literal *literally*' as a 'vogue word', giving no clear explanation of why, in his view, some common uses are 'vogue' or 'clichéd' (bad), others, 'integral' and 'legitimate' (good).
† Legal formulas such as *cease and desist* and *null and void*, designed to prevent undesired interpretations of the law, are yet another story.

architectural parlance, 'rear elevation'. Now, however, *forefront* essentially means 'front front'. Thus 'X is at the forefront of efforts to do Y' could perfectly well be reworded 'X fronts efforts to do Y' or 'X is at the fore in efforts to do Y'. Does anyone care about the redundancy built into *haphazard* or *forefront*? Not for the first time: no.

Despite the many doubled uses that the gripers accept, they *believe* they find redundancy idiotic, flinging about such dismissive labels as *tautological*, *pleonastic* and *prolix*. They may allow the odd *over and above* to pass without remark, but reject a 'positive role model', 'free gifts', anything 'times tenfold', and a 'self-confessed' anybody. Bill Bryson gets going on *old adage*, 'An adage is by definition old'; *first conceived*, 'Delete "first"'; *from whence*, '*Whence* means "from where"'; and so on. Present the grumblers with *workable solutions*, and they will wonder about your views on *unworkable* ones.* Remind them to take their *personal belongings* as they leave a Tube carriage, and they will try to imagine what their *impersonal* belongings might be. (And if the answer that suggests itself to them is their casual litter—spent chewing gum; scrunched up shopping lists and receipts—they will then wonder waspishly, is it acceptable to leave such stuff behind?)

You probably already dot your English with a selection of these ready-made redundancies. But in a campaign to expand the range of Good English, that is not quite enough. You need to understand that the gripers see beyond this, and are also permanently poised to pounce on more drawn-out examples—those that qualify for the label 'syntactic pleonasm'. Who among us is at all

---

* Some of those who broadcast lists of pleonastic uses object that an *action plan* provides nothing that is not provided by a *plan*. But most writers and other natural fans of beditation will immediately grasp that there most certainly is a contrast with the all-consuming *inaction plan*.

times and for ever above the odd spot of excitable excess? Mr Bryson himself fires a piece of advice at his readers curiously worded thus: 'On the whole, however, the use of more words than necessary is almost always better avoided'. Is he joking? It is hard to know what 'almost always' contributes to his remark that 'On the whole' has failed to establish. A favourite—which is to say widely derided—form of syntactic pleonasm is any such pile-up that includes the word *both*. In *British Enterprise Beyond the Seas*, 1867, where J. H. Fyfe discusses the different challenges facing shepherds and stockmen in 'Our Antipodes', he writes, 'There are, however, two grave dangers which both share in common'. The sneery rejoinder here would be: why not simply, 'There are, however, two grave dangers facing both'?* Another favourite pile-up can be dated at least as far back as an 1878 report by the New Hampshire Department of Agriculture: 'the reason why is because the price of labor, taxes and farming tools are so high'. 'The reason is X'? 'Why this is, is X'? 'This is because X'? (The price *is*?) More unusual examples also sometimes jump out. In 1917, the Columbia professor Calvin Thomas wrote, about training novelists within universities, 'all the criticism and historical scrutiny and professorial opinionation will do the aspirant no harm if he has a rugged individuality of his own'.† Acidly the griper will wonder quite how an aspirant could ever be conceived of as having the rugged individuality of somebody else.

Some of the more popular forms of pleonasm come across as shameless noise, not least a tag like 'Save up to 70% off', where the first word and the last are seemingly doing the same job. Others appear more calculating. Beauty companies, to avoid blunt untruth, often resort in their advertising copy to pleonastic

---

* Under the heading 'number' in his style guide, Mr Bryson notes, 'Both of the following examples come from the same issue of *The Times*'. So it goes.
† *The Unpopular Review*, Vol. 7, 1917, p. 150.

assertions that are hard to unscramble, as for instance in this strapline from the cosmetics company Lancôme: 'Wrinkles appear visibly reduced'. The thought of X merely 'appearing' to be *visibly* Y is hard to fix in one's mind. What is being promised here? Impossible quite to say.

In C. S. Lewis's *Studies in Words*, he defines 'verbicide' as 'the murder of a word'. The offence happens, he says, 'in many ways. Inflation is one of the commonest; those who taught us to say *awfully* for "very", *tremendous* for "great", *sadism* for "cruelty", and *unthinkable* for "undesirable"'* were verbicides'.† One might respond to this that if the senses of the words Lewis regretted really were dead and gone, at least the lexical corpses left behind in this process were successfully zombified—back up out of their graves at once, if they were ever in them, and pumped with the lifeblood of new meaning. How does this stack up against the efforts of the gripers to annihilate what they consider nasty neologisms?

Many hundreds of years ago, in *Troilus and Criseyde*, Chaucer pointed out that words prized in the past can come to seem 'nyce and straunge', and yet, he added, the fact is 'thei spake hem so'. They did indeed; and much of Chaucer's own vocabulary is now of course nice and strange to us in turn—for example, he used *nyce* to mean 'rare'. Nobody knows what the tides of future language change will bring, nor what they will take away. But change

---

* In *One Word and Another*, 1954, V. H. Collins declares boringly (and without due reflection) that 'the statement that anything is unthinkable is self-contradictory'. Picking up this torch, John Humphrys, in *Lost for Words*, rules that it is wrong to describe as 'incredible' that which we can believe.

† Lewis did not come up with the term *verbicide*, nor was he the first to use it to describe a word-killer as opposed to the crime of killing words. The *OED* dates *verbicide*, in both its senses, to the middle of the nineteenth century, but actually there is an entire (comic) lecture on the subject 'by a man of the law' in the *Monthly Magazine* for April 1826.

itself is certain. Do not be cowed by the violent talk of the gripers; and especially, do not be too *precautious* in the face of their ver-bicidal instincts. They may *firefight** 'barbarous vocables', but if it suits you, and as long as these words still have their dash of power, why should your language not be *skyrocketty, incredible, awesome*?

* '. . . constantly firefighting practical, commercial and ethical problems' (*Guardian*).

monumentous

While we are on the subject of fluctuating values, bear in mind that another way to tease the gripers is by being vague with words of number and measure. The annoyance a precisionist is capable of feeling when faced with this form of misuse is exemplified by the following remark, taken from the work of Wilfred Whitten and Frank Whitaker: '"To a certain extent" means to an uncertain extent'. Does it really? The *OED* explains, in what might be thought the ugliest way possible, that this use of *certain* indicates an amount 'particularized' but 'left without further identification in description', and it gives numerous examples of this meaning, starting in the 1300s.

Griping about uncertain *certain*s may not be as fashionable as it once was, but there are many people today who get comparably steamed up about the supposed misuse of *myriad*. The *OED* supplies a definition from 1555: in line with the word's Greek origin, it explains that 'One myriade is ten thousande'. In English, however, as the *OED* also points out, *myriad* has always simultaneously meant 'an uncountably large number', and not even the most defiant of pedants would say that a car valued at ten thousand pounds was worth 'myriad quid'. No one would say that, yet keen gripers, faced with the remark 'I saw a myriad of fireflies' refuse to hear 'I saw a great number of fireflies'. Instead they will insist that in such a sentence, *myriad* should be used as an adjective, 'I saw myriad fireflies', thus embracing the possibility, no matter how remote, of their number having been 10,000. Those same gripers would presumably also baulk at the report of a journalist who wrote, 'Tourists from myriad countries all filed into the lobby and respectfully took photos of its interior from a distance' (*Guardian*). By any normal measure, there are about 200 countries in the world. To a precisionist, therefore, this description must suggest in the order of 9,800 countries (and goodness knows how many tourists) too many, lending the description a hysterical air.

Confused? Yet more inflammatory to those who care about these matters is the sloppy use of *decimate*. Simon Heffer has strong views. After starting, 'As every schoolboy knows',* he goes on to explain that 'decimation' was a Roman military punishment 'in which every tenth man was killed'. This is true. But it is also true that the first meaning in English of *decimation*, when it came into the language in the fifteenth century, was the taking of a tithe—a tax of one-tenth—because from the fourth century on, the verb *decimare*, in ecclesiastical Latin, had been used to refer to tithing.† *Decimare* is found with this meaning in the Vulgate, so that what St Jerome gave as 'qui decimatis mentham, et anethum, et cyminum' (Matt. xxiii. 23)—and what the Authorized Version would later give as 'for ye pay tithe of mint and anise and cumin'—Hugh Latimer, in 1549, in a sermon delivered before King Edward VI, could give as 'decimations of Anets seade, and Cummyn'.‡ The fiscal understanding of *decimate* persisted in English for centuries; there is even evidence of the word *decimator* being used to mean a tax collector. But Mr Heffer, having declared that

---

* Lucky them.
† The word *tithe* is itself rooted in the Old English word meaning 'tenth'.
‡ Latimer was burnt at the stake by Mary I in 1555, in part because of his beliefs about the fitting uses of English.

decimation is a word contemporary speakers 'insist on wrenching from its correct etymology', concludes that its 'correct sense in English' is the 'reduction of a body of people by 10 per cent'. If that ruling were somehow correct, it would have been alarming news for the subjects of a sentence in Daniel Neal's 1738 work *The History of the Puritans*, Vol. IV, in which he notes Cromwell's resolve that all those who 'declared themselves of the Royal party, should be decimated'. Helpfully for us, Neal explains what he intended by this: 'that is, pay a tenth part of their estates'.

Those unnerved by Mr Heffer's crushing declarations will be correspondingly glad to find lined up against him a noted historian, a great Protestant martyr, and one of the most revered and intellectual of all the Christian saints. Yet the fuss among our advisers about what *decimation* really involves is more commonly focused, not on who or what is reduced, but on the exact amount of that reduction. As some schoolchildren might indeed suspect or even know, in origin the 'dec' in *decimate* relates to the value 10; and yet for more than three centuries, *decimate* has been used to mean 'inflict heavy damage upon', with the tacit implication that, although the destruction of a tenth part might be pretty bad, the toll in question is vastly worse. Among all classes of griper, this vague but violent use of *decimate* is a source of despair, especially when the figure of one-tenth is directly flouted: 'The number of wild animals on Earth has halved in the past 40 years, according to a new analysis. Creatures across land, rivers and the seas are being decimated . . .' (*Guardian*).

But why do the gripers care so much about this particular example of a slide into vagueness? After all, English provides many other words whose specific values have been altered in defiance of their etymology, with the purist high horse nowhere to be seen. The noun *journey*, for instance, comes from the Old French *journee* or 'day', and in English was used from the thirteenth century to mean 'a day's travel'. As a measure of distance, the *OED* explains, this was taken to equal about twenty miles, so that 'iurnes two' in 1325 meant roughly forty miles. (A *mile* itself, or the early Old English *mil*, is derived from a Latin unit of distance measuring a 'thousand' paces.) Some time after *journey*'s travelling sense was established, it began to be used also to mean 'a day's labour', making a *journeyman* a day-labourer. And *journey* would come to be used in other day-specific ways as well. However, from the mid fourteenth century on, the ostensibly tautological expression a 'day's journey' began to creep into the language: the idea had arrived that other durations for a 'journey' might be possible—with what lumbering, imprecise results in current usage we know only too well. Imagine how much more incredible *The Incredible Journey* would have been had the pets made it home across the Canadian wilderness in twenty-four hours flat!*

Similarly, the original, seventeenth-century definition of *quarantine*—like *decimate*, a word ultimately derived from the Latin—was a forty-day period during which a widow had the right to remain in the property of her deceased husband. (The desert where Christ fasted for forty days and forty nights was given the name Quarentena.) But what of *quarantine* now? Can it be true that we have allowed its modern meaning to be dictated to us, not on pure etymological lines, but according to the rate of progress of a variety of deeply unpleasant diseases?

Even *heaps* started out as a specific measure, a fixed 'heap' size, before the Earl of Surrey chose to write, in 1547, so depressingly loosely, 'what heapes of joy these litle birdes receave'. The *OED* credits Shakespeare with, all of a sudden, in *Troilus and Cressida*, converting *loads* from being specific to non-specific, when he

---

* Perhaps in these circumstances John Humphrys, who would rename *The Incredible Journey* 'The Credible Journey' (see p. 136), might be willing to revert to the original title.

wrote of the hell of 'loads o' gravel i' th' back' (*gravel* meaning kidney stones). In 1575 or thereabouts, a *lot*, too, ceased to be used exclusively for a specific portion, when John Hooker wrote, 'The next day the people, like a lot of wasps, were up in sundry places'. This particular corruption was still inspiring heroic resistance three hundred years later in *Don't*, the 1883 manual by 'Censor' that we met in Chapter 11: one of its helpful instructions is 'Don't say "lots of things," meaning an "abundance of things." A *lot* of anything means a separate portion, a part allotted. Lot for quantity is an Americanism'.*

The tidal pull of vagueness continues, and has heaved more recent terms out of position, including a combining form from the 1960s, *nano-*. It is a fair bet that few of the people who now fling *nano-* about know, or would particularly care, that scientists dreamt it up to represent the value of one thousand-millionth: almost at once it took on the convenient meaning of 'quite amazingly small'. Those, conversely, who insist on referring to etymologies will be arrested by the knowledge that *nano-* is drawn from a Greek word for a dwarf.

You might think that with all the examples above of early-onset imprecision, *loads*, *lots*, *myriads*, *heaps*, and so on, English would have no need of further imprecise terms of quantity. Yet seemingly from nowhere, the nineteenth century coughed up loads more, among them *smidgen*, *scads* and *oodles*. The word *umpteen* has suggested 'an impressive number' for over a century; then came *yonks* and *gazillion*. But if these six non-words are horrible, none of them is likely to be thought *more* horrible than three further examples that deserve a quick mention. We met earlier (p. 76) the term *ginormous*, coined by British servicemen in the

---

* 'Censor' was the pseudonym of Oliver Bell Bunce—an American. He also wrote bullishly: 'Don't say "loads of time" or "oceans of time." There is no meaning to these phrases'.

Second World War. It achieves its sense of childish over-inflation by blending two pre-existing size-words with the same rough value, *gigantic* and *enormous*. *Humongous* (however one spells it) works in much the same way, suggesting *huge* with perhaps a dash of *monstrous* or *stupendous*. The *OED* passes the haughty judgement on *humungous* that 'probably' it is 'factitious', whatever that is supposed to mean. It was, even so, the very word wanted one day by a writer who cannot possibly be called lax. Saul Bellow, a great mixer-up of language, found a place for it in his last novel, *Ravelstein*: '. . . years went by, and it became apparent that I was unable to begin, that I faced a humongous obstacle'. Perhaps Bellow wanted to borrow a note of childlike defeat or awe.*

Humungous and *ginormous* bring to mind a word that would doubtless be found even stupider by the huffers and puffers, and the only one of these three that the *OED* has not yet deigned to include on its pages: *monumentous*, a nifty blend of *monumental* and *momentous*. As long ago as 1890, Sir Arthur Conan Doyle gave it a whirl in the speech of a character in his novel *The Firm of Girdlestone*: 'in all his experience he had never met with a more "monumentous episode"'.†

On top of this wanton multiplying of size terms, there is yet another form of imprecision that disconcerts the gripers, namely the careless use of false singulars and plurals—which may sound complicated, but is common enough. Arguments about whether the Latin plural *data* can legitimately be used in the singular in English are so tedious that they can cause one to lose the will to

---

* If *humongous* was the word that suited Bellow in this sentence, then R. H. Fiske, having declared that *ginormous* 'does nothing to improve our understanding of ourselves or our world', is on a sticky wicket when he calls the 'hideous, ugly' *humongous* 'equally silly, equally loathsome'.

† Another, simpler word ready-made for widespread revulsion, if only more people knew about it, is *hugeantic*, as here: '"All is cool, my hugeantic friend"': Daniel James Miller, *Window in Time: Shifters, Book 2*, 2014, p. 100.

live; and on this, even stalwart guardians of Good English have given way (though not the *Economist Style Guide*, which insists that *data* is plural while noting its 'almost universal' use as singular). Bill Bryson, for variety, takes a stand against treating the Greek-origin singular term *kudos* as a plural, but all in vain: 'The Douglas letter concluded with a kudo to Justice Blackmun'; 'geographical territories were mentioned for honors and various kudos given'.* And why stop there?

> The bio-data of each personnel is duly maintained in the data bank.

> An Unidentified Remain is defined as: A body of a deceased person or any part of a body known or assumed to be human . . .

> 'I'm giving you ten seconds to begin clearing the premisis!'†

The grumblers will not grumble so much as storm at 'a *personnel*', 'a *remain*', 'a *premisis*'. Yet, as ever, there are precedents for this kind of madness, absorbed by English centuries ago, that we more than tolerate today. Both 'a *cherry*' and 'a *pea*' are ancient misconceptions derived from foreign words that were already singular, *cheris* and *pease*. And the singular *asset* was born from a misunderstanding of the Anglo-Norman legal term, also singular, *asez*, meaning 'enough property'. No more satisfactorily, the plural endings on *invoices*, *trousers* and *tweezers* were added to forms already plural, or treated as plural, *invoys*, *trews* and *twees*. What next, one might wonder, *invoiceses*, *trousersers* and *tweezerzez*?

---

* Bernard Schwartz, *A History of the Supreme Court*, 1995, p. 350; James M. Comer, *Sales Management: Roles and Methods*, 1977, p. 208.
† See S. N. Chand, *Dictionary of Commerce and Management*, 2006, p. 35; Government of Canada website: 'Canada's Missing'; Red Jordan Arobateau, *Jailhouse Stud*, 1977, p. 92. Superfast Worcestershire online, meanwhile, explains captivatingly that broadband speed 'is affected by the distance that a premise is located from its serving cabinet'.

Perhaps not, especially given what we encountered in Chapter 1, the 'illusive' but greatly desired 'perfect trouser'. It might cross your mind to wonder why, if *trousers* is to be pared back down to a single plural, the *r* should be left on the end, instead of the spelling being *trews*, or, to conform to modern norms, *trouse*. But then this whole area is a muddle. Why, for example, does Marks and Spencer, selling singular *knickers*, have a '*Knicker* Style Guide'? The answer seems to be that when 'bipartites' are used in a compound, we drop the *s*. For this reason, it is a '*trouser* press' in which we press our *trousers* (if we do), and we are told to fear a visible '*panty* line' though it is caused by our *panties* (supposing we wear them).

Most of us treat all of this as being of vanishingly little consequence, and the language certainly stands it, as it stands much that is peculiar and illogical. Even our foremost gripers—though, like Hooker's wasps, they are 'up in sundry places'—seem bothered by only a few of the oddities among English words of number and measure. Still, to promote your cause, if you are keen, you could use some of the unaccommodated examples above. And if your reputation has the least *remain* at this point, it should soon have shrunk to absolutely nothing at all.

PART II

'In short, he who would fail must avoid simplicity like a sunken reef, and must earnestly seek either the commonplace or the *bizarre*, the slipshod or the affected, the new-fangled or the obsolete, the flippant or the sepulchral.'

ANDREW LANG, *How to Fail in Literature*, 1890

ON REGISTER

viscera, vitals and pluck

In George Eliot's novel *Middlemarch*, Fred Vincy explains to his sister that 'All choice of words is slang'. 'It marks a class', he says, and then adds, rather brilliantly: 'correct English is the slang of prigs'. The word *slang* dates from the mid eighteenth century. It started as a low term for low terms—an example of what it named. But by the 1870s, when *Middlemarch* was published, its meaning had widened in line with Fred Vincy's definition, so that it could also be used to suggest the special vocabulary of a particular group—what Elizabeth Griffith, back in 1766, had referred to as a 'privileged Dialect'.

We shall not detain ourselves here with how the prigs managed to nab the labels 'correct' and 'good' for their particular form of slang. The fact is that they did. And it is in a spirit of dauntless righteousness that they continue to dismiss the English of others as uneducated, convoluted, genteel, abominable, and so on. John Humphrys, in *Lost for Words*, speaks with unabashed good spirits of a use that 'we' shun because 'it would make us sound common'. Simon Heffer, as we have seen, condemns a grammatical norm exemplified by Louis Armstrong on the grounds that it is 'vulgar'. But a linguist would agree with Fred Vincy's thesis that Louis Armstrong's English is one sort of slang or dialect, and that of Messrs Humphrys and Heffer, another.*

A person could simply try to ignore the stresses and strains of worrying about this sensitive aspect of usage. And sure enough, most people, most of the time, comfortably do. But if you are ready to take on the gripers, and would rather not fight blind, what follows?

In the shadow of this question lie the great, fraught realms of 'register'.

Our choice of verbal register is, in the most general sense (as *register* has for some decades been interpreted), our choice of the type and grade of our language in relation to the circumstance in which we are using it. This may see us conforming to an understood dialect of a sort: 'journalese', 'teen-speak', 'business English'. It may also require us to pay close attention to the degree of formality we employ, on a scale usually depicted as running from high to low. And most of us are attuned to numerous registers (going with the loose definition above), whether we recognise this in ourselves or not. So it is that we juggle our words to fit the occasion, making them hyperbolic, cagey, crude, vague, obsequious, American, and so on, as somehow feels appropriate—or as feels productively inappropriate.

---

* The standards of correctness promoted by arch-gripers are a challenge even to those who set huge store by them. For instance, Mr Heffer advocates a slightly outmoded version of what would be called in the trade 'formal Standard English', but, being human, can forget himself even when it comes to the basics. Take an article of his in the *Daily Mail*, 15 November 2013: he writes 'JFK was the first politician to fully embrace the black arts of image manipulation . . .'. Yet in his style guide he warns his would-be followers against the split infinitive as 'inelegant'. Of using *they* as a singular pronoun, he booms, 'I regard that as abominable and want no part of it'. Yet in the same *Mail* article he continues: 'Until JFK, top-class politicians were chosen for their wisdom and devotion to their country. Now, it is someone who can perform a flirtatious interview with a breakfast television dolly bird, irrespective of what they say'.

Because we can draw these distinctions, it is possible to set up a clash for effect. Two radically contrasting registers are captured by the *OED* in the definition it gives for its undated third sense of the verb to *bog*. Picture the exercised lexicographer writing that to *bog* is a 'low word, scarcely found in literature, however common in coarse colloquial language'. 'Low', 'common', 'coarse' and 'colloquial'! Unusually for the *OED*, no supporting quotation is given to illustrate this gutter-bound use of *bog*, from 'literature' or anywhere else; all we get is the withering assertion that it means to 'exonerate the bowels', or 'defile with excrement'. The meaning of 'defile with excrement' couched in the register of *bog* itself would seem to be to 'shit on'. Meanwhile, use of the verb *exonerate* to mean 'discharge' is clearly marked elsewhere in the *OED* as long obsolete. Evidently, scaling the heights of language register by means of a rarefied archaism allowed the lexicographer to 'exonerate' the dismay of having to work on *bog* at all; or, put another way, it apparently gave this person the comforting sense of having bogged *bog*.

Questions of register can be more subtle than this. *The Economist Style Guide* advises its readers not to use *participate in*: 'use *take part in*, with more words but fewer syllables', it says. On the facing page it gives the advice to avoid *come up with*, proposing as an acceptable substitute *originate*. If a consistent standard of judgement had been applied, it would have been necessary here to say the exact opposite: 'with more syllables but fewer words'. Why the contradiction? What the guide sees no need to explain—indeed, might find it hard to explain—is that, in the register of English that it favours, *come up with*, but not *take part in*, ranks as too informal, while *participate in*, but not *originate*, sounds a shade prim.

If few people fret ceaselessly over just how to pitch what they say, most will from time to time put *some* thought into the matter, not least because English so often supplies us with a choice of more than one word for more or less the same thing.* The shades of difference between overlapping terms can be slight. For instance, little distinguishes *fury* from *rage*. Yet what of *intestines*, *entrails* and *guts*? If you were to stab a knife into any of these you would cause identical harm; but that does not mean that these three words, in what they refer to, do the identical job. The 1858 original of *Gray's Anatomy* is full of uses of *intestines* but has not a single use of either *entrails* or *guts*. And though the text does carry the odd allusion to 'the gut', it never uses the word *gut* in a heading. At the other end of the scale, has anyone ever acted on 'intestine instincts'? Could a person 'bust an entrail' to finish a job on time?

There are other words that overlap in meaning with the three above: *innards*, *vitals*, *bowels* and *viscera*, for example, as well as *splanchnic* (usually an adjective) and, in origin, *pluck* of the kind a brave person can be said to show (*pluck* being a term for the guts 'plucked' from a butchered carcass). This gives us more ways of naming the digestive tract, and potentially some other stuff inside the torso, than most of us seem to require; and indeed, *splanchnic* would probably elicit from the average person today, 'Sorry—what?' In a 1382 translation of the Bible, two Old English words are formed into a compound to create yet another term for our list: 1 Sam. v. 9 is given as 'the arsroppis of hem goynge out stonken'. Even disregarding the quotation's religious source, it is pretty startling today to read this unapologetic reference to someone's 'arse-ropes' going out stinking.† But these many words, with their shifting connotations, all have, or have had, their uses, and can be compared for usefulness now—the trouble being that

* Whole books are given over to waxing philosophical about the relationship between words and what they name, but we shall glide right past this question, merely acknowledging that it exists.
† The Authorized Version gives instead: 'and they had emerods in their secret parts'.

not everyone faced with a choice of overlapping terms will come to the same conclusion about how each is best used.

Another squib from Alfred Crowquill's 1854 *Electric Telegraph of Fun* (whose 'don'ting' we met in Chapter 5) concerns pitiful qualms in this very area. Under the mocking title 'Elegance', Crowquill writes, 'A lady who wished some stuffing from a roast duck, which a gentleman was carving at a public table, requested him to transfer from the deceased fowl to her plate some of its *artificial intestines*'. Elsewhere in his compendium, Crowquill ridicules a second lady—who might as well be sister to the first—for chiding her little son when he seeks to read a 'tale' out of the newspaper, not a 'narrative'. The boy promptly urges the nearby house-dog Sancho to stop '"shaking his narrative!"'

It is a similar scene in *Middlemarch*, of domestic speech being policed, that provokes Fred Vincy into making the declaration given at the head of these remarks, that 'correct' English is no more than its own form of slang ('the slang of prigs'). He throws out this quip because his sister, Rosamond, has just reproved their mother for referring, not to the 'best' of the young men of Middlemarch, but to the 'pick' of them—*pick* classed by Rosamond as 'vulgar'. The 1956 film *High Society* has an exchange conducted in much the same spirit, when a conservative matron scolds her daughter for saying that she is 'pooped' rather than 'enervated': the moviegoer is left in no doubt that the kid is *pooped*. Has anything changed now that the twenty-first century is well under way? In what was a widely reported story, the powers that be at Harris Academy, Upper Norwood, felt themselves compelled in 2013 to produce a list of words 'banned' from use in the school's classrooms and corridors. They included *like*, *extra*, a throat-clearing *basically* and the terminal *yeah*.

You may well fully grasp the difference between *pooped* and *enervated*, and yet find yourself in a slight fog about how to use register in your campaign to broaden the scope of Good English.

It is true that here matters do become mildly confusing. After all, if the gripers deem more than one register to be unpleasant, as they do—yielding what they consider to be gross failures of style—does it not follow that there must be more than one wrong register for a dedicated misuser of English to choose from?

It most certainly does! Indeed, there will always and in every circumstance be many more wrong registers available to you than it is possible to count, so that we could hardly dream of studying them all even if we wanted to. Happily for us, however, no such course of study is here required. Instead, we shall confine ourselves to looking at the handful of registers that our advisers appear to hate the most. Which of these you might then like to attempt, and when, will be up to you.

19

FANCY LANGUAGE

clinquant ansation

It is a widely agreed principle of Good English style that a person should not write too 'high'. Francis Grose's *Classical Dictionary of the Vulgar Tongue*, splendid repository of eighteenth-century London street-slang, unsurprisingly contains several entries hostile to vocabulary lying at the other end of the scale. A *binnacle word* is defined as 'a fine or affected word', one 'sailors jeeringly offer to chalk up on the binnacle' (the box that houses a ship's compass). *Break-teeth words* are 'Hard words, difficult to pronounce'. And *word grubbers* are 'persons who use hard words in common discourse'. Fair enough. Yet in the history of lexical mud-slinging, it is not Grose's low speakers alone who have taken this stance. Francis Bacon, revered essayist, in his 1625 remarks on 'Vain-glory', is no less hostile to fine or affected language when he translates a French proverb into the English form '*Much bruit,** little fruit*'. A century or so later, in his famous work *An Essay on Criticism*, 1711, Alexander Pope laid down more precisely—in heroic couplets—the following observation: 'As Shades more sweetly recommend the Light, / So modest Plainness sets off sprightly Wit'. And a century after that, William Hazlitt, yet another venerated essayist, in a *Table Talk* reflection of 1822 'On

* 'Noise' (used as a verb in the expression to *bruit abroad*).

Familiar Style', would disparage verbal immodesty once again: 'Any one may mouth out a passage with a theatrical cadence, or get upon stilts to tell his thoughts', he said; it was all too easy 'to use a word twice as big as the thing you want to express'. Indeed, from Shakespeare's blinkered Holofernes criticising one who 'draweth out the thread of his verbosity, finer than the staple of his argument', to V. H. Collins in 1956 decrying 'the show words of the sham erudite'—and beyond—the disdain for fancy language is the same.

But what exactly are these too-big, fancy 'show' words, and where do they come from?

It does not take much idling through back numbers of the *Provincial Medical Journal* to find that on 7 February 1844, an unhappy vicar was driven to send a letter from his 'very retired' Lincolnshire village in protest at recent changes to medical vocabulary. Warming to his subject, the poor cleric then commented on a wider fad for over-classicising and Frenchifying ordinary English. His honest barber, he said, had been succeeded by a *peruquier* (French for 'wig maker'). Instead of soap, this *peruquier* fellow was selling *rhypophagon* (Greek for 'dirt-eater'). Rather than 'spatterdashes'—forerunners of spats—the wretched local saddler had started to sell *antigropelos* (Greek for 'against wet mud'). And the list goes on.* Most people would probably agree even now that *peruquier*, *rhypophagon* and *antigropelos* come across as a bit much: 'horrid barbarisms', the oppressed vicar calls them. He, however, could not conceal his kinder nature, concluding at the last, 'I suppose it was a little innocent vanity'.

Though French and Greek are the ultimate source of a good number of our break-teeth words, Latin is always held up as guilty of supplying more. A hundred years after Hazlitt argued

---

* As it happens, *barber* is itself derived from the French; but *soap*, *spatter* and *dash* are all Germanic in origin.

for the merits of a familiar style, Fowler, in his *Dictionary of Modern English Usage*, popularised the notion of some words being 'genteelisms'—if not twice, then at least one-and-a-bit times 'as big as the thing you want to express'. As Fowler himself explained it, a genteelism was not the 'ordinary natural word', but a synonym 'thought to be less soiled by the lips of the common herd, less familiar, less plebeian, less vulgar, less improper, less apt to come unhandsomely betwixt the wind and our nobility'. He listed among his examples using *assist* rather than *help*, *cease* rather than *stop*, *expectorate* rather than *spit* and *proceed* rather than *go*. In each case, this is a warning against a word with its roots in Latin.

Fowler was by no means the first to deprecate this special, slightly elevated, Latin-inflected register. In *Middlemarch*, the language of Mr Borthrop Trumbull, auctioneer, attracts comment from the narrative voice in the text, when he remarks, '"I have just been reading a portion at the commencement of 'Anne of Jeersteen.' It commences well"'. Parenthetically, the narrator notes, '(Things never began with Mr Borthrop Trumbull: they always commenced, both in private life and on his handbills)'.*

But is it really so wrong to use *commence* for *begin*, and if so, why? Ambrose Bierce, in 1909, ruled on this very point when he described *commence* as 'not actually incorrect, but—well, it is a matter of taste'. Kingsley Amis, taking his turn on the topic, was no more helpful. The two were more or less synonymous 'in a way', he said, and then added, without explaining: 'only someone with no feeling for words would treat them as interchangeable'. The dusty definition of *commence* that even now lingers in the *OED* similarly draws unflattering comparisons with *begin*. *Commence*, which came into English in 1320 via Old French, is the

---

* Should you doubt the flick of scorn here, it is confirmed by Eliot's rural rendering of the title *Anne of Geierstein*, a novel of 1829 by Sir Walter Scott.

'more formal' of the two, the *OED* states; it classes the Germanic *begin*, three centuries older, as being 'native', and therefore 'preferred for ordinary use'.*To see *commence* marked as not-so-native after it has been in the language for 700 years may strike the casual reader as odd; yet the prejudice laid bare here, and still held up by the *OED*, has seeped into twenty-first century thinking as well.

Genteelly opting to *commence* rather than *begin* is only one type of Latinate English at which those from the school of modest plainness look askance. In 1824, in his novel *Redgauntlet*, Scott (again) defined *slang* as 'thieves-Latin', meaning, it seems, the obscure tongue of the underclass. To this it is worth observing in reply that *actual* Latin has often supplied the obscure slang of the ruling classes—by some lights, the very definition of thieves themselves. A shabby evasiveness marks many of their Latin-heavy uses even today: job cuts explained as *readjustments*; aerial bombing raids said to have resulted in *insurgents* being *degraded*; such opaque expressions as *interpolated terminal reserve, liquidity constraints, dematerialised securities* and *extraordinary rendition*. Nor could a Lincolnshire vicar of our own time, no matter how retired, suppose that it was merely 'a little innocent vanity' that led the American intelligence agencies to start referring to a *disposition matrix* when they meant what the rest of us would call their 'kill list'.

Who might be excused the use of hard words? A philosopher, maybe? Bishop Berkeley declared in 1713 that although his writings were there to be 'thorowly understood', by goodness you could expect to have to work at it. 'I may perhaps be obliged', he said, 'to use some *Ambages*, and Ways of Speech not common' (*ambage*, from the Latin, is in origin a term for a circumlocution;

---

* This is to prefer what used regularly to be called our 'Anglo-Saxon' vocabulary over words, mostly Latin in origin, that entered our language mostly after the Norman invasion.

it came to us via the French, where it picked up the further meaning of a quibble or an ambiguity). But even if one were to cave in and meekly grant that obscure terms might be essential to an obscure subject, what of the 'word grubber', the person who, in the dismissive definition supplied by Francis Grose, uses 'hard words in common discourse'—or who, in Hazlitt's way of looking at things, exhibits 'arbitrary pretension'?

A keen student of the works of Will Self will soon be equipped to dream of *prefructive viridity*, *intercrural fulguration*, *ensorcelled abulia*, and other wonders. But not every passing newspaper reader who alights on one of Mr Self's articles is going to be prepared to labour in order to take his meaning. Mr Self's own response to these presumed lexical minnows is that they are 'anti-intellectual' and represent the 'banal middlebrow'*—to which the banal, anti-intellectual, middlebrow object of his scorn can but vouchsafe the silent reply (presumably in Mr Self's view woefully latebrous[†]) that it obumbrates[‡]—and so lumbers with tiresome cunctation[§]—even the most aliped[¶] of arguments to have it served up in an altitonant** style;—and further, that Mr Self's more snogly[††] chosen words are mishits so fraught with aliety[‡‡] that they must leave obcaecate[§§] analphabets[¶¶] aerumnous,*** and on the

---

* See 'A Point of View: In defence of obscure words', *BBC Magazine*, 20 April 2012.
† 'Full of lurking holes'.
‡ 'Makes more obscure'.
§ 'Delay'.
¶ 'Nimble'.
** 'Thundering from on high'.
†† See Nathan Bailey's *Universal Etymological English Dictionary*, 17th edn. (1757): '*snogly geer'd*, handsomely dress'd'.
‡‡ 'Otherness'.
§§ 'Deficient in spiritual insight'.
¶¶ 'Illiterates'.
*** 'Full of trouble; wretched'.

evidence *do* leave some positively estuating,* their thoughts, not elevated, but inspissated† with agelastick‡ resentment.

A second 'banal' or 'anti-intellectual' point might be this: that when readers come upon a word they have never previously encountered, and one that they do not then find to be used by anyone they ever meet—say *ensorcelled*§ for *bewitched*—it will permanently lack, as Hazlitt puts it, 'precise associations', or in other words, subtlety in how it plays into register—with the inevitable consequence that its effect will be that of a blunt instrument, not a weapon of refinement.

By now you may be mentally placing yourself among the minnows, determined to keep your choice of words as modest as possible. You are perhaps repelled by the impenetrable slang of the oppressors, some of whom must justify so much more than their love of classical euphemisms. You, at a venture, staggered through the run of ambages above. Fine—and yet if you wish to oppose the gripers in their rigid declarations about what constitutes Good English style, you must at least consider the advantages to your cause of an over-uppish register.

The immediate thought might be that you should commence *commencing, opining, residing, proceeding, apprising*, and the like. The least bias in your English towards this primly Latinate vocabulary will attract the contempt of what Addison called 'your little Buffoon Readers'.¶ And if you draw the fire of your foes by this means, with all their strictures on what is 'preferred for

---

* 'Roiling like the sea'.

† 'Thickened'.

‡ 'Morose'.

§ 'I was immediately ensorcelled by the singularity of the Shrigley worldview': Will Self, *Guardian*, 18 October 2013.

¶ *The Spectator*, 25 May 1711. (Of course, there are innumerable Latin-origin words that no griper objects to or even notices: *perplex, obliterate, necessary, relinquish, associate, preliminary, redolent, counter-productive, triumph* . . .)

ordinary use', you will be showing solidarity with the many poor souls who totter in your wake—today's Borthrop Trumbulls, who so doggedly trade in these words even now, and in the process helplessly defeat themselves in their desire to command a modicum of respect.* Given your aims, this would be an honourable and good-natured course for you to take—but be aware that in promoting this mildly elevated register, you would be joining a war of attrition that you could not reasonably hope to live long enough to win.

Possibly a more desirable course of action would be to attempt to unnerve your enemies by aping those writers who are prepared to be fancily incomprehensible. This is not as hard to pull off as you might imagine. A word grubber like Will Self must privately sweat over the question of whether or not he is a fine user of his fine lexicon, and thus a good guide to writing with it well. You, however, are blessedly free of the need to entertain yourself with such worries. Milton stirred himself to invent *intervolve*, *horrent*, *omnific*, *displode* and *pontifice*. You have merely to turn to a reasonable dictionary and it will supply you with countless such words that hardly anyone knows offhand how to define, or even dimly recognises. Nor do you need to present yourself as a latter-day Bishop Berkeley, choosing *clinquant*† vocabulary as a way to give helpful *ansation*‡ to your arguments (whatever *they* may be). No, your drift into the world of ambages will be in pursuit of something far simpler—what in *Daniel Deronda* George Eliot called 'the odour of departed learning'. True, with this musty

---

* In his 1720 'Letter to a Young Gentleman, lately enter'd into Holy Orders', Swift listed as a fault typical of young clergymen—but one of which anyone might be guilty—the frequent use of elevated words, known 'by the better sort of Vulgar', he says, as 'fine Language'. Mr Borthrop Trumbull is the better sort of Vulgar.
† 'Spangled'.
‡ 'A supplying of handles'.

insult to the nostrils you will dismay just about everyone—from seething gripers, through the 'banal middlebrow' (if there is a difference), to those who wrap their thoughts in common, coarse, colloquial, low English. But it is above all the gripers who will be thrown off by your copperplate obscurity. They may vaunt a plain style, but faced with break-teeth words, they will sneakingly fear that they have been outsmarted at their own game: the game of knowing best. What—they will wonder in a panic—if these are the show words, not of the sham erudite, but of the *actually* erudite—of those who know *even better*? Once you have knocked them off their perches, and have them temporarily at your mercy, who knows what you may not achieve? As our man Hazlitt disapprovingly observed, 'When there is nothing to be set down but words, it costs little to have them fine'. Friend, go ahead and help yourself.

20

MONOSYLLABLES

zap

The widely held prejudice that we have just examined against a style too tinted with Latin is echoed in a sweeping comment by Thomas De Quincey, author of *Confessions of an English Opium Eater*, in an 1845 essay he wrote on William Wordsworth. Here De Quincey argued that what he called 'lyrical emotion'—emotion concerning our most profound feelings—could be captured in none but our oldest words, because, as he put it, 'the Saxon is the aboriginal element'.

This is a popular view even now. By being only moderately selective, one can point to a divide between the punchy 'Saxon' or Germanic underpinnings of today's English, and our insipid Latin-based uses. Take a few instances of common combinations of words. Many examples in the language have exclusively Germanic roots, *free love*, *dog days*, *fire storm*, *blood lust*, *death wish*. Are these not more 'significant and emphatical', as Nathan Bailey puts it in his dictionary, than the recent Latinate confections *sanitary product*, *stabilisation unit* and *structural deficit* (not to mention *liquidity constraints* from the previous chapter)? It could even be argued that by juxtaposing a word ultimately of Latin origin, and an 'aboriginal' English word, we can make subtle use of the contrast between the two, as for example in *mission creep*, *urban sprawl*, *counterblast* and *military strike*, or, to reverse the order of word-origin, *snap decision*, *fear factor* and *death sentence*.

And yet might it not be that what makes these contrasts seem persuasive (assuming they do seem persuasive) is the fact that in the examples given above, all the 'aboriginal' words, and only those words, are monosyllables?

The prejudice expressed by De Quincey goes hand in hand with a rough-and-ready belief that our oldest words are our shortest, a view reinforced by little lists that get bandied about showing, for instance, how (to return to a group we have already considered) the Latin-based *intestines*, from the early 1500s, has three syllables; *entrails*, of around 1300, and coming to us via Old French, has two; while *gut*, from around 1000, and of Germanic origin, has one. Yet if you take *field*, *star* and *nail*, all of which have been in our language for well over 1,000 years, and add a Latin-origin monosyllable to each, to give, say, *force field*, *pole star* and *nail bomb*, do any of these come over as somehow less 'emphatical' than *field-fresh*, a putatively seductive label used to promote frozen vegetables; *star dust*, a sort of something supposedly emitted by celebrities; or *nail care*, chemically dizzying as it may be—three pairs of monosyllables fully 'aboriginal' in their constituent parts? Is the Latin word *lax* in some mysterious way outdone by its Viking equivalent, *slack*? In short, does it really matter whether or not 'words monosillable', as George Puttenham put it in *The Arte of English Poesie*, 1589, 'be for the more part our naturall Saxon English', or should we now weigh up the monosyllable as a thing 'entire of itself', to be judged regardless of where it comes from?

Let us say that it does *not* matter to us, and that we shall do exactly that.

The force of the monosyllable, and the esteem in which, on the evidence above, monosyllables appear to be held, could lead to the easy assumption that as a class they will fall within the bounds of Good English—making them, to a misuser, a lost cause. If long words are suspect, are our shortest ones not bound to be the very thing? Well, not necessarily, is the answer to that.

Indeed, there are arguments strewn across the history of reflections on English that go entirely the other way. Thomas Nashe, in his 1594 riposte to his reprehenders, wrote strongly on the subject. 'Our English tongue, of all languages, most swarmeth with the single money of monasillables, which are the onely scandal of it. Bookes written in them, and no other, seeme like shop-keepers boxes, that contain nothing else save halfe-pence, three farthings and two-pences.' He continues: 'Therefore, what did me I, but having a huge heape of those worthlesse shreds of small English in my *pia mater's* purse, to make the royaller shew with them to mens eyes, had them to the compounders immediately'. As we saw in Chapter 8, Nashe's half-pence attitude gave rise to his compound coinages *chatmate, potluck, homespun,* and so on. At least he got something out of his contempt—as did we.

John Donne, in sermons written a few decades after Nashe dashed off his piece, was, if anything, even less tolerant of these 'worthless shreds', discussing more than once what he presented as the disproportionate power of some of our smallest words. In a New Year's Day sermon of 1625, for example, he declared, 'It is an Execrable and Damnable Monosillable, *Why*; it exasperates God, it ruins us'. Addison put a braver face on things in a *Spectator* essay of 4 August 1711, when he noted that 'by its abounding in Monosyllables' English 'gives us an Opportunity of delivering our Thoughts in few Sounds'. It is tempting to point out that those sounds are all the fewer for the fact that some monosyllables carry a dazzling array of meanings. *Pad*, for instance, simply as a noun, has since the twelfth century been used to denote a toad, a frog, a hidden danger ('a pad in the straw'), a track or path, a starfish, a highway robber, an elephant's saddle, the launch point for a rocket, a lily leaf, a bachelor's flat, and more. And between them, *stump* and *stock*, to pick another two, have covered almost more meanings than one can count. But for all that, Addison was not in the end favourable. 'I have only considered our Language as it shows the Genius and natural Temper of the English,' he wrote, 'which is modest, thoughtful, and sincere, and which, perhaps, may recommend the People, though it has spoiled the Tongue'. Shortly after this, Swift, also unimpressed, wrote that English is 'overloaded with Monosyllables, which are the Disgrace of our Language'.

Perhaps the very lowest point of this 'disgrace' fell at the end of the 1700s, as laid out in a number of editions of Grose's *Classical Dictionary of the Vulgar Tongue*. Here, numerous slang terms are glossed in the same way. *Tuzzy-muzzy*: 'the monosyllable'; *Bottomless pit*: 'the monosyllable'; *Mother of all saints*: 'the monosyllable'; *Eve's custom house*, *Black joke*, *Watermill*, *Brown Madame*, *Miss Laycock*: all 'the monosyllable'. Anyone innocently mystified by Grose's euphemistic explanation of these euphemisms, who therefore looked up his definition of the word *monosyllable* itself, would have found it explained as 'a woman's commodity'. Those, by contrast, who knew enough to check the *actual* monosyllable to which Grose referred, given in the second edition of his dictionary as 'C**t', would have found it defined for them as 'a nasty name for a nasty thing'.*

All of that having been said, it was not the identification of the monosyllable with that much celebrated 'nasty' thing, the 'C**t', that most worried those commenting on monosyllables in years gone by. Instead, a great deal of the debate centred on their metrical quality. Dryden wrote in 1697, in his translation of works by Virgil, 'It seldom happens but a Monosyllable Line turns Verse to Prose'. An anonymous reviewer of Cowper's

---

* *Thing*, itself a monosyllabic alternative to Grose's politer *commodity*, is first known to have been used to refer to a person's private parts by Chaucer, courtesy of the Wife of Bath, in the expression 'thynges smale'. The *OED* recognises *thing* in this sense, but not *commodity*—and sadly not *monosyllable* either.

translation of Homer wrote similarly in 1793 that 'the most vig-
orous attempt' to convert a mellifluous tongue into English will
frequently be baffled by 'The hoarseness of Northern language
bound in pebbly monosyllables'.* And Pope agreed. He believed
that 'Monosyllable-Lines, unless very artfully manag'd, are stiff,
languishing and hard'. In a humorous shot at demonstrating
what he simultaneously asserted, he wrote, 'And ten low words
oft creep in one dull line'. He does at least include the caveat 'oft'
here. Was Shakespeare on poor form in all the sonnets that he
began with ten monosyllables—including number 42, 'That thou
hast her, it is not all my grief'; 75, 'So are you to my thoughts as
food to life'; and 141, 'In faith, I do not love thee with mine eyes'?
Was it 'languishing and hard' of Yeats to start one of his most
treasured poems: 'When you are old and grey and full of sleep'?

Even a critic fully persuaded that these lines are dull and flat
would be hard-pressed to deny that great writers of English glory
in the capacity of its monosyllables to set off longer words, in
poetry and in prose. It is difficult to say how the men who wrote
the Authorized Version of the Bible could possibly have bettered
the terrible question 'My God, my God, why hast thou forsaken
me?' And Shelley, to pluck a lyrical poet out of the air, makes no
less dramatic a use of contrasting syllable-counts in the words of
his famous rallying cry from *The Masque of Anarchy*, written in
response to the Peterloo Massacre:†

> Rise, like lions after slumber
> In unvanquishable number,
> Shake your chains to earth like dew
> Which in sleep had fallen on you—
> Ye are many—they are few.

---

* *The Analytical Review*, Vol. XV, January 1793, p. 2.
† On the word *Peterloo*, see p. 75.

And is it by chance that there is only one word that is not a monosyllable in the following much-loved, deliberately sing-song lines from Philip Larkin's 'This be the Verse'?

> They fuck you up, your mum and dad.
> They may not mean to, but they do.
> They fill you with the faults they had
> And add some extra,* just for you.

The fact is that English monosyllables are not all always automatically hoarse, pebbly, low and worthless. And some are as elevated as any word can be. The author of the great fourteenth-century mystical work *The Cloud of Unknowing* recommends that if you wish to pierce that cloud, as it separates you from God, you must fasten a word to your heart 'so that it never go thens'. But how? 'Take thee bot a litil worde of o† silable; for so it is betir then of two, for ever the schorter it is, the betir it acordeth with the werk of the spirite. And soche a worde is this worde GOD or this worde LOVE.'

The debates above about the value of monosyllables may seem like very old news, but we remain contradictory about them even now. To ask a person to put something 'in words of one syllable' is to say, in effect, 'be clear and get to the point'. It is this sort of thinking that leads *The Economist Style Guide*, under the heading 'short words', to write: 'Use them'. At the same time, a person described as being 'monosyllabic' is implicitly uncommunicative and possibly even gruff. The hostility underlying this second take on our shortest words is reflected in the work of R. H. Fiske, his *Unendurable* reflections including this one: 'If you speak

---

* See p. 153 for the attempted banning of the word *extra* by Harris Academy, Upper Norwood (though not on account of its being too Latin).
† 'One'.

in monosyllables you likely* think in monosyllables. Complex thoughts, well-reasoned arguments, a keen understanding of self and society—each and all of them lost, squandered, forfeited'.

But where does all this leave your campaign to introduce a fissure into the defences set up around Good English? If you choose to disregard Mr Fiske's jeremiad by favouring monosyllables, do you not run the risk of producing the plain, strong style recommended by *The Economist*?

By a winding route, we find ourselves back at the question of register. Shorn of any context, there are monosyllables that it might be thought would sit some way up the scale: *vouch*, *shrift*, *dint*, *traipse*, *zeal*, *thwart*. There are others that will appear plain and necessary: *sing*, *dog*, *leaf*, *life*, *if*, *but*, and so on. No normal griper would object to a word of either class in the flow of a Good English sentence. But where our advisers do identify misuse of monosyllables is in the pages of most newspapers, especially in a headline of the type 'Drug-probe ploy backfires'. You may be thinking that this style of headline is a special case, a 'privileged Dialect', in the words of Elizabeth Griffith, and not a worry for anyone else. But Simon Heffer, among others, disagrees. When it comes to the common tongue, 'No-one', he writes, 'can discount the effect of the tabloid press'. Though he believes that we should, in the main, 'stick to simple words', *tabloidese* is where this all goes wrong—and in going wrong, he argues, supplies a 'fuel that feeds the vice of exaggeration'.

It is certainly true that tabloid headlines are designed to be compact come-ons, and that the words chosen for the job are often pebbly with the undifferentiated force of *blast*, *stun*, *roast*, *pan*, *maul*, *zap* or *slam* for *counter*, *oppose*, *condemn*; of *bid* or *push* for *attempt*, *endeavour*, *foray*; of *key* for *important*, *necessary*, *central*;

---

* *Likely* used to mean 'probably' is classed by *The Economist Style Guide* as one of its 'horrible' words, but here Mr Fiske is true to himself as an American.

of *ploy* for *stratagem, system, device*; of *rap* for *suspicion, accusation, indictment*; of *foil* for *impede, frustrate, defeat*; and of, in addition, *rats, babes, tots, cheats, scams, curbs*, and more. Monosyllables drawn from this list and dropped into a headline often act as cartoonish substitutes for the text they supposedly represent. In 'Hacked nude pix: Google zaps links' (*Guardian*), *zaps* stands for 'has removed two'. In 'How milk zaps tooth decay' (*Daily Mail*), *zaps* represents 'can neutralise'. In 'Fpl Chief Zaps Enron Deregulation Push' (*SunSentinel*), *zaps* turns out to refer to the efforts of a senior official who has been 'taking a dig at' plans for deregulation. In 'Our boys zap Syria' (*Sun*), *zap* means 'have been bombing'.

This use of monosyllables as a casual shorthand clearly contributes to giving them a bad name, but some of them have a bad name anyway. Mr Heffer categorises *posh, dosh* and *scam* as 'pure slang', and says that they 'have no place in respectable writing'. He would surely have added *zap* to this list if it had occurred to him—not to mention *biff, bop, bonce, dweeb, bint, nix* and *faff*. In short, individual monosyllables, as much as any words, can end up being identified with particular registers, so that in an otherwise unexceptionable piece of Good English, some of our shortest words would supply a wild blip of tone.

If, however, monosyllables, just as other words, can carry this sort of load, it follows that how each one rates is potentially open to change. In 1954, countering the usual trend in these matters, V. H. Collins was able to describe the two-syllable, Latin-origin noun *present* as a 'more natural and simple word' than the Germanic monosyllable *gift*. He added, 'Those, however, who draft advertisements prefer gift, and so do the genteel, especially perhaps women'. Would those who still favour *present* over *gift* agree with the last of Collins's fine discriminations? And would they also agree in decrying (as he did) the use of *stress* to mean 'emphasis', or *dire* to mean 'dreadful'? The sensitivities that led him to dismiss *stress* and *dire* as 'vogue-words' have long since withered away, suggesting that others of our low monosyllables might one day be brought within the sweep of common-or-garden Good English too.

However forcefully the gripers attempt to contain the language of everyone else, their lexicon does, over time, change. A word they at first find blunt may come to acquire nuance, and one they once thought low may make its way up in the world. If you should happen to wish to fill your *bonce* with 'complex thoughts, well-reasoned arguments, a keen understanding of self and society', go ahead. In doing so, it is true, you will *zap* the proprieties of the gripers—but who can say how this will end? Hold your nerve, friend. Give it a whirl. Seize the day.

21

BOVRILISATION

ikr

There are souls lingering in the world who, at the drop of a hat, and with relish, will still recite the whole of 'A for 'orses, B for mutton, C for miles, D for rent', etc.,* but who are dismayed to be put to reading *n* for 'and' or *k* for 'okay'; or *kk* for 'yes, absolutely: got it'. There are those who have put *RSVP* on countless invitations, who use *etc.* (as above) without a blush, who speak of *TLC* and shake with laughter telling you (again) about the boy called R. W. C. Smayles, who nevertheless despair at being told that *l8rz* means 'until later', or that *ikr* means—anything at all (I know, right). In a much-cited article in the *Daily Mail*, 24 September 2007, John Humphrys asseverated (as he might perhaps rejoice in one saying) that those 'vandals' who use 'grotesque abbreviations' in their text messages are 'pillaging our punctuation; savaging our sentences; raping our vocabulary'. 'Text-speak', he explained—the putting of *u* for *you* or *4* for *for*—was 'destroying' our language; and it was therefore a type of English he longed—or believed he longed—to see abolished.

There are many types of word shortenings, some of which we

---

* That is, 'Hay for horses, Beef or mutton, See for miles, Different . . .'. The 'Cockney Alphabet' dates back at least to the 1940s, and there must be many versions of it tucked away in odd corners of the minds of our older citizens: '. . . X for breakfast, Y for mistress, Z for effect'.

have already met. Mr Humphrys would doubtless also blench at, for example, the *Guardian* headline cited in the previous chapter, 'Hacked nude pix: Google zaps links', a headline the *Guardian* itself decided to rewrite. But does anyone object to the shortened form *photos** with which the word *pix* was eventually replaced? And what of the example *TLC* above? Most people would describe this as an 'acronym' (a term coined in the 1940s), because *TLC* is made up of the first letters of 'tender loving care', though many linguists draw a distinction between 'abbreviations' as a general term for a word made from the beginnings of other words, and the two types, the 'acronym', where a pronounceable word results, e.g. *fomo*, 'fear of missing out', and an 'initialism', e.g. *e.g.*, where the letters are said in succession. An initialism may contain convenient vowels and yet still be too much of a mouthful to enunciate as a whole word, as is the case with the teaching union the *NASUWT*. Meanwhile, some acronyms achieve their whole-word status by borrowing beyond the first letter of the words from which they are derived, for instance *Soweto*, or 'South Western Township'. Without this practice, the National Biscuit Company, *Nabisco*, would have been *NBC*. With it, *NBC*, the National Broadcasting Company, could have been 'Nabroco'. (Though these two companies dodged a clash, there are innumerable examples of competing uses of a single form, such as *PTA*, used for both 'parent–teacher association' and the 'Prevention of Terrorism Act'.)

An acronym like *Soweto*, or *laser*,[†] may become so settled in the language that we rarely think of it as an abbreviated form. And even an initialism can come loose from its origins. These

---

* *Photo* is classed by linguists as a 'clipped' form of *photograph*.
† 'Light Amplification by Stimulated Emission of Radiation'. (There is an argument that the second word here ought to be *oscillation*, but this gives rise to the unfortunate acronym *loser*.)

days it is increasingly common to see reference to an entity's 'USP' as though this means simply its 'rationale', 'thang' or 'that which makes it a bit special'. But *USP*, a term devised in 1961 by business theorists, originally shortened the phrase 'unique selling proposition'—the last word often now reinterpreted as 'point'. In more recent use, a *USP* may very well not be 'unique' in the literal sense of the word, and may not concern selling in the commercial sense of 'selling' either, making the word *proposition* questionable as well.

As we have seen, these abbreviations are not the only types of shortened words to litter the language. In Francis Grose's *Classical Dictionary of the Vulgar Tongue*, he explains 'P. P. C.' thus: 'An inscription on the visiting cards of our modern fine gentlemen, signifying that they have called *pour prendre congé*, i. e. "to take leave." This has of late', he continues, 'been ridiculed by cards inscribed D.I.O. i. e. "Damme, I'm off"'. *PPC* may mean little to most of us today,* though *i.e.* (*id est*) is still going strong. But what of 'Damme, I'm off'? This phrase, too, has its shortened forms, contracting the longer 'Damn me, I am off'. The oath *damme* may be long gone,† but it is hard to believe that there can be more than a handful of contemporary speakers of English who permanently eschew the contracted form *I'm*.

In 1953, Paul C. Berg noted uncontroversially that English words had been being pruned by 'unknown gardeners of the language' for centuries. They had been, still are being and doubtless will be for centuries to come. The Domesday Book, medieval masterpiece and a founding text of British history, is a wonderful compendium of Latin abbreviations. *Mr*, contracted from *master*,

---

* To some, however, it will mean 'pay per click' or 'peripheral pin controller'.
† It was once so popular that the term *dammy boys* was used to mean 'delinquents'. Byron saw fit to provide this gloss in *Don Juan*: '"Damme's" quite ethereal, though too daring— / Platonic blasphemy, the soul of swearing'.

is first found in 1447.* The shortened form *fan*, from the 1680s, meaning broadly an 'admirer', is derived from the word *fanatic*, a century and a half older. And *mob*, according to the *OED*, was first recorded in 1688. This shortening, perhaps of the phrase *mobile vulgus* but certainly of the word *mobile*, quickly took hold as a term for a non-static rabble inclined to acts of lawlessness, so that by 1695, one Charles Hatton could write familiarly in a letter that 'For thes 2 nights a great mob have been up in Holborn and Drury Lane'.

In the eighteenth century, many notable writers took a stand against words pared down in this manner. Though Swift's private 'little language'† contained numerous examples of forms such as 'nite' for *night* and 'Ppt' for *poppet*, he did not scruple to parody in public what he saw as a verbal habit of the fashionable fool. In a letter he composed for *The Tatler* in 1710, he mocked a style that he represented as being more abbreviated than whole: 'I *can't‡ do't*, that's *pozz*—*Tom* begins to *gi'mself* Airs'. And in a later work, *A Complete Collection of Genteel and Ingenious Conversation*, he again derided, among other 'Abbreviations exquisitely refined', 'Pozz for Positively, Mobb for Mobile, Phizz for Physiognomy, Rep for Reputation' and 'Hipps, or Hippo, for Hypocondriacks', as well as 'Bam for Bamboozle' ('and Bamboozle for God knows what', he added).

A sense of muddle between abbreviations useful, entertaining and condemned can be found across the period. In 1709, Richard Steele kept readers of *The Tatler* amused by reporting that an honest gentleman from out of town could not understand the remark 'Do not talk to me, I am Voweled by the Count, and

---

* For the record, it was *Mr* that gave rise to the word *mister*, not the other way round.
† See Chapter 12.
‡ The contraction *n't* for *not* was then fairly new: Swift was against *n't* as well.

cursedly out of humour': the sophisticated Londoner of the day knew that to 'vowel' someone was gambling slang for paying a debt with an IOU. Francis Grose, to tickle his own readers as they lexically slummed their way through his dictionary, explained the slang phrase 'Moll Thompson's mark' by saying, 'M. T. i.e. empty: as, Take away this bottle, it has Moll Thompson's mark upon it'—a sort of pseudo-abbreviation. And Thomas Gray, author of 'Elegy Written in a Country Churchyard', a poem widely revered as the quintessence of Englishness and one of the beauties of the language, was cheerfully willing to butcher the word *visit* in a letter of 1767: 'Tomorrow I go vizzing to Gibside to see the new-married Countess'. In the previous sentence, he had spoken of being at Hartlepool and 'visiting about', a common phrasal verb at the time. If, in visiting about, he had happened to maunder through a local churchyard, and had read a tombstone or two, he would almost certainly have encountered slews of highly contracted forms: 'Eliz Relict of Edwd'; 'of much Honr'; 'Feb ye 9 An Dom 1753'; 'who depd this life'.*

Shortenings abounded in the eighteenth century even among the dead, and yet we find Addison, in *The Spectator*, in the same frame of mind about them as Swift: 'It is perhaps this Humour of speaking no more than we needs must which has so miserably curtailed some of our Words'. He points out: 'they often lose all but their first Syllables, as in *mob. rep. pos. incog.* and the like; and as all ridiculous Words make their first Entry into a Language by familiar Phrases, I dare not answer for these that they will not in time be looked upon as a part of our Tongue'. *Vizzing* may never have gained a hold, *incog* for *incognito* is now pretty recherché, and *pos* or *pozz* did not survive in common use either. But

---

* Would Mr Humphrys, idly rubbing the lichen off an old headstone, wax wroth at these forms too, calling them 'grotesque abbreviations' and an antique 'raping' of our vocabulary?

the miserably curtailed *mob* is of course fully 'part of our Tongue'. And *rep*, too, persists, though it still feels like a shortening. It has stood for the word *reputation* from the early 1700s on, but to a modern ear may well sound much more recent, making it seem to sit oddly in a line of Fielding's from 1732: 'Nor modesty, nor pride, nor fear, nor rep, / Shall now forbid this tender chaste embrace'.*

The nineteenth century saw a similar mixed bag of responses to shortened words. The *zoological gardens* of 1829 would soon exist without difficulty in tandem with the *zoo*. The word *cits* was used to refer reductively to *citizens*. The *telephone* became a *phone* as early as 1880. And naturally a joke was still a joke. In Crowquill's *Electric Telegraph of Fun*, he describes how a young girl, asked her favourite letter of the alphabet, replies, '"Well (blushing and dropping her eyes), I like U best"'; and in 1840, the *Comic English Grammar* had the line 'A blow in the stomach is very likely to W up'. But there were also Victorian gripers—and how, so that the same book, at the very end, warns its readers archly: 'Never, under any circumstances, let the abbreviation "gent." for gentleman, escape the enclosure of your teeth'. The *OED* has yet to revise its embarrassing definition of *gent*, which explains the ban with unconstrained snobbery: 'now only vulgar, exc. as applied derisively to men of the vulgar and pretentious class who are supposed to use the word, and as used in tradesmen's notices'. With even greater force, and perhaps slightly more reason, an 1877 leader in *The Times* would rail against the clipped language of the telegram as a 'barbarous makeshift', explaining that 'Gushes, sighs, tears,

---

* In 1749, Fielding wittily defined a *demirep*, literally a 'half reputation', as a woman 'whom everybody knows to be what nobody calls her'. In the 1890s, *rep* came to stand for *representative* as well, as in *sales rep*; and in 1925, for *repertory*, as in *rep theatre*. But despite these rival meanings, crooks and gangsters carry their dubious reputational 'reps' to this day.

sallies of wit, and traits of fondness, do not stand the ordeal of twenty words for a shilling, and the frigid medium of unsympathetic clerks'.

Even as this diatribe went into print, a Scotsman called John Lawson Johnston was dreaming up the beef extract Bovril, its name derived from parts that suggest bovine virility,* or a sort of dumb potency, perhaps worryingly unstoppable. Bovril was an immediate success; and in tribute, for several decades after its invention, boiled-down language would come to be described despairingly as 'bovrilised' English. There were various places beyond stock 'cablese' where the public found bovrilising to be expedient. One was the advertisement columns of the newspapers, which in the Victorian period were full of truncated forms. For instance, in advertisements for governesses, either required, or seeking employment, it was common to find writing of the sort: 'XPD teacher', 'Ex. refs.', 'reduced terms (40 gs. per annum)', 'resident Fr. and Germ. govs.', 'clergyman's Dtr', 'desires Re-ENGT'. This was also the era of what we now call 'shorthand', including systems of single-sign abbreviations sometimes referred to by those who first devised them as 'grammalogues'.

In our own time, gripers bore on about *PIN number* on the grounds that it can be said to denote 'personal identification number number' (as *ATM machine* yields 'automated teller machine machine'). Those who make this point never mention what they feel about *D-Day*, which shortens 'Day-Day', nor do

---

* The second half of the name Bovril was more directly taken from Bulwer-Lytton's novel of 1870, *The Coming Race*. This strange work concerns a super people whose force stems from 'vril', glossed in the text as 'the unity in natural energic agencies'. But take a step back, and Bulwer-Lytton's coinage sounds awfully like a compacted version of the Latin-derived *virile*, a reading of the word made the more plausible by the fact that he called a female of the 'coming race' a 'Gy', and a male, an 'An', evidently clipped versions of the Greek *gyne* and *aner*.

they explain whether they recoil from talking about 'an' *RSVP*, and so on. And it is not only old codgers who worry about bovril-ised forms sinking too comfortably into the language; young codgers have their worries too. Some of them object to *peeps* as a shortening for *people*, as, to them, it suggests (or they feel that strictly it ought to suggest) *peoples*, which means something else. There is also youthful crowing over those who write 'HIFW when'. *HIFW* is short for 'how I feel when', as *MRW* is short for 'my reaction when', and *MFW*, for 'my face when', so that the person who adds a whole-word *when* at the end (and who is not being annoying on purpose) is taken to be stupidly writing 'how I feel when when', etc. Premature codgeriness also afflicts those who find objectionable the use of *looooool* to mean 'laugh out loud (for quite a long time without stopping)', spurred by the idea that this ought instead to mean, or in the words of one *Guardian* commentator 'actually means', 'laugh out out out . . .'.*

Perhaps an old-style griper stalking the pages of this book would laugh out out out loud to think of tribes of online bovril-isers snarkily monitoring one another in this way. But it is not surprising that many of them do. The internet is full of English that has been altered in order to dodge automatic filters and, no less importantly, to keep outsiders at bay, and this is fertile ground for displays of linguistic one-upmanship. A general label for one simple substitution code often used to distort online English is *leetspeak*, otherwise rendered as variations on *1337SP34K* (using numbers to approximate the appearance of some of the letters). No doubt everything about the word *1337SP34K* would disgust a griper, though it happens that using *leet* as a shortening of *elite* is nothing new—which is to say that it dates from 1441, by the *OED*'s reckoning, and an era when to be 'on the leets' was to be

* *Guardian*, 28 May 2014.

among the elect. And of course substitution codes are nothing new either. The guardians of Good English will presumably never encounter online leetspeak at its most developed and impenetrable, but from time to time, as John Humphrys's outburst confirms, they are very likely to stumble across popular formulas of a similar kind, in texts, in advertising slogans and on car number plates—*b4* for 'before', *4eva* for 'for ever', *wuu2* for 'what you up to?', *qt3.14* for 'cutie pie', *M9* for someone who is slightly more of a mate than is signified by *M8*. And if these, one and all, are ghastly, what of 'An Essay to Miss Catharine Jay'? *Dwight's American Magazine* printed a version of this poem—which has delighted people ever since—back in 1847, of which the following is a representative sample: 'From virtue never D V 8; / Her influence B 9, / Alike induces 10 derness, / Or 40 tude divine'.

tl;dr:* everyone uses shortenings, but many shortened forms are tribal. For some people, this is a world of the *CofE*, of a *cuppa*, of *plane* tickets and going *awol*; for others, more of *apps*, *bots*, *sth*, *ofc*,† *ffs*, and worse. Was Charles Dickens defeated in his desire to become a great master of English prose because he happened to be a whizz at shorthand? Is text-speak really destroying the English of the young?

As an out-of-work Victorian governess might have put it, the gripers are happy to X Qs the crime of bovrilising when they commit it themselves, but are liable to be disquieted or contemptuous when left on the outside by the shrivelled words of a

---

* This bovrilised rendering of the phrase 'too long; didn't read' (or alternatively, 'too *lazy*; didn't read) is usually used either as a wearied response to being presented with dense text, or as an alternative to the old-fashioned phrase *in sum*. Though old-fashioned writers may find even the second, more helpful use of *tl;dr* abrasive, they will perhaps send up a cheer on discovering evidence of modern abbreviators standardising a use of the semicolon.
† 'I live in a place where reading is sth only nerds do and is like a crime'; 'Yes ofc I will'.

different gang. If you run even slightly ahead of them, they may well defensively class you as 'not all that'—though all that *what* they will feel no need to say. Eighty years ago, A. P. Herbert preached against 'the imbecile "O.K."' If he could be revived, *k*, *kk*, or the meditative version *mkay*, would presumably finish him off all over again. It is inevitable that our own gripers will fight with Herbertesque vigour to keep such shortened forms out of today's Good English. But if you ignore their strictures, *U* or *UR* lexical heirs will definitely score some wins in the end. *L8rz*.

22

MACARONIC HOO-HA

disploded yawps

Pope, in *An Essay on Criticism*, wrote, 'In words, as fashions, the same rule will hold; / Alike fantastic, if too new, or old'—which sounds great, except that we all cheerfully use numerous words that have been in service for over a thousand years, and take up at least some newly formed words with scarcely a blink.* It might, therefore, be truer to venture that our language risks seeming alike fantastic, if too high, or low. Hazlitt certainly formed this conclusion when he argued for the 'familiar' style, saying that 'It utterly rejects not only all unmeaning pomp, but all low, cant phrases, and loose, unconnected, slipshod allusions'. What he did not mention is that, while pavonine† pomp and bovrilised cant are taken by the restrained stylist to be equally unappealing, putting pomp and cant together produces a style that a griper can be expected to find considerably more disagreeable than either on its own.

It may be that in special circumstances an argument can be underscored by using a controlled mismatch of registers. We saw on p. 151 how a lexicographer, required by the *OED* to define

---

* In 1946, Whitten and Whitaker noted (what it would no longer quite be possible to say) that 'Some words become fashionable on a sudden, like some table-decorations or a particular breed of dog'.
† 'Peacock-like'.

the colloquial verb to *bog*, did so in an excessively formal manner as a way of indicating scorn. Mark Twain took a similar
approach, though to much more genial effect, after noting
(see p. 15) his 'steadily-increasing pleasurable disgust' at a terrible
piece of writing. He added: 'I will remark, in the way of general
information, that in California, that land of felicitous nomenclature, the literary name of this sort of stuff is "*hogwash*"'. Twain
manages to make the cant term *hogwash* appear all the more of
an insult by dressing it up in the Latin frills of 'felicitous
nomenclature'.

But it is not always as clear as in the two examples above why
a writer has chosen to bump high against low. The author Will
Self protested publicly in 2012 that the mingled style of his prose
was just what he was after, and he seemed to propose in the process that the right intercutting can provide a kind of balance. He
explained that in defence of what he called his 'obscure' vocabulary,
he had been wont to point out (until giving up on arguing about
it altogether) that his sentences were 'as full of resolutely
Anglo-Saxon slang as they were the flowery and the Latinate'—as
though words splendidly from the first category can somehow
cancel the evil of words less splendidly from the second.* It is
true that he likes to go for a mix. In a recent article on the vanished Berlin Wall, he described 'its anguiform length wriggling
through the city'.† *Wriggle* we all know. This word has never stood
on ceremony, or stilts. According to the *OED*, it first appeared
in English in 1495, in the sentence 'The adder Alphibena ...
glydeth and wryggleth'. It came into our vocabulary from Low

---

* *BBC Magazine*, 20 April 2012. (In the *Guardian*, 12 February 2015, Mr Self
inexplicably criticises another author for 'Employing a sort of "low baroque"
prose', citing the phrase 'cantillating with gusto'—singing zestfully—as an
example of what he condemns.)
† *Guardian*, 10 October 2014.

German, and is related to *wiggle*—the *-le* on the end of *wriggle* and *wiggle*, and indeed *waggle* and *wobble*, being a 'frequentative' suffix, or one that suggests a repeated action. Let us agree that Mr Self was being no more than mildly fanciful when he used *wriggling* to describe a wall whose very purpose—once up and until it came down again—was to stand still. Fine, but where does that leave *anguiform*? 'Wriggling', for all of its long history in our language, starting with the adder Alphibena, has been associated with snakes. Did Mr Self therefore pair it with *snaky*, or, for glamour, with the more elevated *serpentine*? No. He paired it with a word mugged up out of the Latin and then visited on an ungrateful nation by a nineteenth-century scientist famous for futilely vamping his researches with confected terminology.*

Mr Self's up-down, hybrid style, though unquestionably choppy, is nevertheless thrown rather into the shade by the outpourings of the comedian and social commentator Russell Brand, who see-saws between registers to either maddening or whizz-pop, riproarious effect, depending on the tastes of his audience. In this example from his second 'booky wook', he describes how in the days before he had any fame, he liked to imagine the snowy ravishment of actually getting some: 'vainglorious sycophants will clamour to yawp odes of awe and wonder into my wealthy fizzog while fertile accolades and praise will avalanche the fields of my barren esteem'.

Swift, as we have already seen (p. 175), mocked the word *phizz*, giving it in 1738 as an example of a fad for abbreviations 'exquisitely refined'. Dr Johnson was no more enamoured,

---

* The word *anguiform*, 'snake-shaped', was coined in 1800 by Thomas Young, and has been little used since. Among his numerous brilliant successes, Young contributed to the deciphering of the Rosetta Stone, and proved that light travels in waves. He was renowned for his impenetrable way with words.

describing *phiz* in his dictionary as 'formed by a ridiculous contraction'. (Furthermore, he added crossly, 'if it be written at all', it should be 'phyz'.) But their scorn was not enough to drive it out of the language. In *Mill on the Floss*, George Eliot was able to milk a contrast between the complete and a maimed version of the word when she described the blandly well-favoured Tom as having 'a physiognomy' in which it seemed 'impossible to discern anything but the generic character of boyhood; as different as possible from poor Maggie's phiz'. By the time Eliot was using the squished *phiz* to suggest an imperfect face, there were other variants in play besides. The *OED* credits the first three-syllable version to Coleridge, who wrote in 1791 of 'a very blackguardly fellow, whose phisiog. I did not like', while the two-syllable *physog* was initially clocked—as a 'vulgar abbreviation'—in an 1811 lexicon of 'buckish slang' and 'pickpocket eloquence'. The spelling *fizzog*, used by Mr Brand, can be found from 1825.

According to the *OED*, the first writer to use *avalanche* as a verb (as in 'avalanche the fields of my barren esteem') was, by strange chance, Mark Twain: 'We avalanched from one end of the stage to the other' (i.e. stagecoach). The words *vainglorious*, *sycophants* and *accolades*, meanwhile, with their roots in Latin, Greek and French respectively, are a good deal closer to the 'pomp' end of the scale than is *yawp*—a staunchly scathing term, cousin to the later *yap*, that came into the language some time around 1400 in imitation of a noisy dog (Thomas Nashe depicts Orion praising the communicative powers of dogs by saying, 'They barke as good old Saxon as may be').* This is all undoubtedly a jumble; but for Mr Brand to use *fizzog*, with its great history of dancing about on the wrong side of the tracks, is

* See *Summers Last Will and Testament*, 1600.

something else again, and demonstrates a particularly impish ear for the language.

Mr Self is often criticised for his prose style, presumably on the grounds that he should know better; Mr Brand, on the grounds—so he believes—that he should know worse: 'I think these columnist fellas who give me aggro . . . for using long words are just being territorial', he writes. 'When they say "long words" they mean "their words" like I'm a monkey who got in their Mum's dressing up box or a hooligan in policeman's helmet.'* Of course, he has as much right to dream of the *accolades* of *sycophants* as the next person, absolutely. But it is not his 'long' words alone that stand out, and it seems at least as likely that the aggro he mentions is provoked by his wanton joying in a macaronic clash of dialects.†

By using every trick in this book—if you were to come out all guns blazing—you too could achieve a macaronic style, one gratifyingly deemed to be even worse than the sum of its parts—*ikr*! Perhaps you feel primed to attempt this even now, and are keen to *displode*‡ across the page a great *wimble-wambling* of *innuendous hoo-ha* cut with *anguigenous*§ words deftly *exfiltrated* from the great back catalogue of English. If so, the result is bound to leave the self-appointed guardians of the language *double-upped* with endless *poultry* objections. And yet, if you really wish to help *evolute* our tongue, *routinising* the *operationalisation* of contested

---

* *Guardian*, 5 November 2013.
† The seventeenth-century adjective *macaronic* shares its etymological roots with the nouns *macaroon* and *macaroni*. It is used to describe writing that represents a hotch-potch of different languages or registers. In his *Comic English Grammar*, Percival Leigh uses another seventeenth-century term for the mixed style when he writes of 'what is called the Mosaic dialect', i.e. languages scrambled to give a result as obscure as Egyptian hieroglyphics.
‡ 'To burst out explosively', possibly sideways. Milton, who invented this word, was not completely clear.
§ 'Begotten of serpents'.

lexicalisations, it is not in the end the gripers whose opinions should matter to you the most. They cannot be avoided, true, and you will have to suffer their scorn. But to prise Good English from their grasp—as they themselves know; and to their endless sorrow—it is in fact every other speaker of the language whom you must endeavour to *understand up, outreach, zap, strike accord with** and *ensorcel*.

* 'Mastery goals with their main focus on understanding and comprehension will strike accord with a deep learning approach': Chi-Hung Ng and Peter Renshaw, in *Research on Sociocultural Influences on Motivation and Learning*, McInerney and Van Etten (eds.), 2002, p. 64

23
IN CONCLUSION

bastards and syllables

Shakespeare has Volumnia, mother of Coriolanus, urge him to placate his enemies by using whatever words will do the job, no matter, she says, that the required words happen to be 'but bastards and syllables / Of no allowance to your bosom's truth'. Perhaps you have a greater respect for your bosom's truth than Volumnia had for Coriolanus's; and perhaps you find that you express yours best in words our advisers reject. If so, you may wish to ask yourself who exactly these gripers are to try to limit what you can say.

There are, however, plenty of people who get by pretty well without using the sorts of words that sit on the average griper's lexical *disposition matrix*. And naturally some of these Good English speakers, finding no need of the extra words, dismiss them out of hand, perhaps agreeing wanly and unscientifically with Swift's conclusion, formed in 1712, that when it comes to the English language, 'its daily Improvements are by no means in proportion to its daily Corruptions'.*

Even if Swift had happened to be right, we all know that out of the apparent swill of new corruptions come numerous words and uses destined to be adopted across the board, so that even the modern gripers whose views we have been consulting brighten

---

* Swift did, though, continue: 'the Pretenders to polish and refine it, have chiefly multiplied Abuses and Absurdities'.

their tomes here and there with 'few authorities continue to insist that', 'only the ultra-finicky would deplore', 'not to seem mincingly donnish',* and so on.

And after all, it would be inconsistent of those who rue the misuses that serve to shrink our language if they were to respond with horror to every last novelty calculated to expand it. The association of error with new possibilities was the point of a remark made by Elizabeth Griffith, when she wrote to her husband in 1766 reporting on the critic of his prose: 'I told him I dared answer for it that you never *confounded Grammar*, though I owned you sometimes puzzled a Dictionary, — and might hereafter enrich one'. (He did. And as a matter of fact, so did she.)

Most of the guardians of what they declare to be Good English advocate a style that is calm, lucid, direct. They do not always achieve these qualities themselves, but we must surely sympathise with them if, in this, their reach exceeds their grasp. It is harder to feel sympathy when, convinced of their own rectitude, they abandon the very civility that they are arguing their Good English is ideally formed to convey. On pedants, Addison concluded in 1711—and sadly here the evidence would seem to bear him out—that 'a great deal of Knowledge, which is not capable of making a Man wise, has a natural Tendency to make him Vain and Arrogant'. This might explain why our gripers declaim on rules when in truth they are discussing fashions, and why they appeal to logic where no detectable logic applies.

In the introduction to this book, we encountered some of the ideas of Richard Grant White, discusser of 'words that are not words'. Expanding on his theme, he wrote: 'Words that are not words sometimes die spontaneously; but many linger, living a precarious life on the outskirts of society, uncertain of their

---

* Bill Bryson is responsible for the first two of these phrases, and Kingsley Amis, for the third.

position, and a cause of great discomfort to all right thinking, straightforward people'. Anyone stilled by the social presumption in this remark of 1870 should be aware that a similar attitude underlies much of what is found in popular style guides to this day.

In the span of time between a novel word or use becoming modestly commonplace and its being so widely circulated that only the mincingly donnish would dream of rejecting it, its standing among those who declaim on the language will mysteriously change. At first it will be dismissed by those who like to get cross about misuses as a product of 'our modern Blunderland'.* But when it is no longer a cause of discomfort to most people, or to even the most resolute of gripers, the gripers will not only accept, all of a sudden, any amount of rule-breaking or illogic in its make-up, but will positively congratulate themselves on being able to celebrate its quaintly idiomatic nature.

There may be a want of coherence to this, and yet the repressive displays put on by our gripers keep many people of a meeker disposition enthralled. If you have ever been advised that you harbour in your English an incorrect use, then you know what it is to be swept up in the great forward march of language change. You could, receiving this wisdom from on high, respond as though stung, and attempt to purify your vocabulary. Or you could decide that there are horrible words you fancy, consider useful and are ready to defend. Why not dot them about the place on purpose? Though you may send the old guard reeling, you will at the same time be contributing to nudging the communal ear. And after all, it is the masses 'in unvanquishable number' who do the real sifting of English; who in the end determine which uses are fated to become serviceable and good. Victorian writers

---

* This phrase was used by William B. Hodgson, professor of political economy at the University of Edinburgh, in his 1881 volume *Errors in the Use of English*, p. 15.

can be found regretting *civilisation*, *unaccountable* and *humiliating*; A. P. Herbert called *motivate*, *reactionary* and *characterise* 'horrible', 'filthy', and so on. These words may not inspire uniform warmth even now, but is anyone still repelled by them?

Each corruption of today that is accepted and absorbed into tomorrow's Good English will be one corruption the less. The threat it currently poses to a griper of inducing apoplexy will be gone; and the menace of griperish contempt for those who favour the misuse will vanish too. Put another way, though if you place yourself among the advance guard you may take some flak, your horrible words will be a gift to your children, your children's children and their children to come.

Before you started reading this little book, you were perhaps not quite clear about the battle lines drawn by our advisers—with all their talk of what is vulgar, abominable and barbaric. And should you find, having surveyed the field, that you have no wish to think further on this subject, you are unlikely to come to any great harm. But the English language is as much yours as it is anyone's: it is one of the wonders of the world that is free. If you choose to, you can play your part in style.

ACKNOWLEDGEMENTS

Boundless thanks to Tanglewest and the mysterious Raymond. Not only were they my companions from first to last while I wrote this book, but they also contributed directly to the text. Via what were, to me, unknown highways and byways of the language, they uncovered material both invaluable and priceless. At the same time, their bracing contempt for some of what I ran past them kept us all amused.

My thanks also to Geoff Pullum, Ida Toth, Julie Barrau and Ingrid Tieken-Boon van Ostade, who very kindly fielded my more outlandish queries; of course they are in no way responsible for what I did with their answers. I am grateful, too, to Katharine Gowers, Timothy Gowers and Helen Small for their generously detailed responses to the MS in its penultimate draft—cleaving, here, to the ordinary sense of the word 'penultimate'.

This book would have been markedly different were it not for the *OED*. I am grateful to all who work on it. I refer repeatedly on these pages to its wisdom; it was my constant resource. I would like to note that it was freely available to me online because I am a member of my local library, in Summertown, which brilliantly struggles on despite every attempt to close it down.

At Penguin, my thanks to Jessica Harrison and to Rebecca Lee, on whom I have learnt to rely—as also to Stephen Ryan, likewise. And special thanks to Tim Waller, best of copy-editors, which I fear he rather needed to be.

Lastly, I would like to thank Eric Griffiths, who, when I mentioned to him what I was up to in writing this book, very sweetly gave me his copy of Johnson's dictionary.

INDEX

A

abbreviations
172–81, 184; in Latin 174

abstract nouns 33, 105–12

acronyms
173; *see also* 'abbreviations'

Addison, Joseph
co-founder of *The Spectator*,
35 fn; on 'fallow' minds, 48;
use of *make out*, 55; *leave off*,
58; on 'murdering' hard words,
89–90; use of *discover*, 115; *none
that is not*, 123–24; on 'little
Buffoon Readers', 160; English
'spoiled' by monosyllables, 165–66;
'miserably curtailed' words, 176;
pedants 189

adjectives
converted, 32–34, 67, 69;
attributive (nouns used as),
33–35, 169; predicative, 33 fn;
gradable, 34 fn; back-formations
derived from, 38, 43; competing
forms, 45; suffixes added to,
98–99, 110–111; formed using-*able*
101–102

adverbs
converted, 31–32, 99; adverbs of
manner, 103; *see also* 'sentence
adverbs'

Ælfric
on *ha ha, he he* 86

affixes
97–104; negative affixes 113 fn

Alfred the Great
use of *outbring, English*, 68;
understand 69

alright
a 'travesty' 77–79

Amis, Kingsley
on *infer, enormity*, 11; *fund* (verb),
28–29; *critique* (verb), 29; *ongoing*,
68; *alright*, 78; *adaption*, 83; *hopefully*,
thankfully, 104; *disinterested*, 118;
irregardless, 126–27, *commence*, 157;
the 'mincingly donnish' 189

Amis, Martin
on *fund, critique* (verbs) 29

'Anglo-Saxon' English
see 'Germanic English'

antonyms
see opposites; *see also*
pseudo-antonyms

aphesis 78

apocope 78 fn, 87

Armstrong, Louis
use of *ain't worth nothing*, etc.
124, 149–50

Augustine, St., of Hippo
use of *orphanus* 20

Austen, Jane
use of *noonshine*, 21; *reticule*, 34 fn;
itty, 90; *liveable* 102

B
baby talk 47, 76, 89–96

back-formations 37–43

Bacon, Francis
on '*much bruit*' 155

Bailey, Nathan
on *abligurition*, *Belly-Cheer*, etc.,
106–7; *snogly*, 159 fn; 'emphatical'
English 163

'barbarous vocables' 4, 137

basically
'banned' 153

Bede, The Venerable
use of *ingo* 68, 70

Bellow, Saul
use of *imbecilize*, 41; *humongous* 143

Bentham, Jeremy
use of *undisfulfilled* 126

Beowulf
use of *fly* (verb), 27; *nother* 81

Berg, Paul C.
on *lovely* (noun), 32; *dieselise*,
Coventrise, etc., 43; *think up*,
dream up, 56 fn; *so what?*, 73 fn;
cinemaddict, 75; 'pruned'
English 174

Berkeley, George, Bishop
on 'ambages', 158; his clinquant
vocabulary 161

Betjeman, John
use of *undismembered* 126 fn

Bible, Authorized Version
use of *ravished*, 128; *unspeakable*,
132; *tithe*, 139; *emerods*, 152 fn;
monosyllables 167

Bible, trans. 1382
use of *arsroppis* 152

Bierce, Ambrose
on *head over heels*, 22 fn;
honeymoon, 25 fn; *jeopardise*, 40;
electrocution, 76; *preventative*, 84;
restive, 100; *literally*, 133 fn;
commence 157

bipartites 144–45

blend words 73–76, 143

bound elements 61 fn, 76, 97 fn

bovrilised English
178–81; on 'bovrilising' 56 fn, 178

Brand, Russell
use of *fizzog*, *avalanche* (verb),
etc., 184–86; on 'long words' 186

Brown, Ivor
on *awful* 132–33

Browning, Robert
use of *nuncheon*, 21; *old-fangled* 117

Bryson, Bill
on *celibate*, 12; *condone*, 19;
miniscule, 23; *finalise*, 41; *lay*, 46;
use of *errors*, 46 fn; on *warn*
(intransitive), 51; *up*, *head up*, 56;
check out, *pay off*, 57; *alright*, 78;
preventative, 84; *viable*, 102;
nauseous, 102–103; *co-equal*,
precondition, 129; *old adage*, *from
whence*, etc., 134; himself
pleonastic, 135; on *kudos* (plural),
144; the 'ultra-finicky' 189

Bueller, Ferris
use of *isms* 108

Bullein, William
use of *text* (verb) 30

Bulwer-Lytton, Edward, first Baron Lytton
use of *vril*, *Gy*, etc. 178 fn

Bunce, Oliver Bell ('Censor')
on *Oh, my!*, *Oh, crackey!*, 86; *lots*, *oceans*, etc. 142

Burney, Fanny
on slipslops, 7–8; use of *Englishize*, *quietize*, 41; *grumpy*, *glumpy*, 74; *skimper scamper*, 94; *frettation* 108

Byron, George Gordon, sixth baron
on Mrs Slipslop, 7; use of *lay*, 45–46; *overtorture*, 68–69; *bah*, 85; *uninterested*, 119; *damme* 174 fn

C
'cablese' 178, 180

Cambridge, Prince William, duke of
use of *babykins* 91

Cameron, David
use of *don't hardly speak any* 125

Carey, Henry
use of *Namby-Pamby* 95

Carlyle, Thomas
use of *conference* (verb) 29–30

Carroll, Lewis
on pretentious abstractions, 32–33; use of *outgrabe*, 69; *mimsy*, *slythy*, etc., 73; on portmanteau words 73–74

catachresis 10

Caxton, William
use of *overhip* 85

celibate
its meaning disputed 12

'Censor'
see Bunce, Oliver Bell

certain
'not certain' 138

Chaucer, Geoffrey
use of *jeopard*, 40; *pass*, 59; on 'nyce and straunge' words, 136; use of 'thynges' 166 fn

Classical Dictionary of the Vulgar Tongue see Grose, Francis

clipped forms 78 fn; 173 fn; 177; 178 fn

Cloud of Unknowing, The
use of *unknowyng*, 118; on *God*, *Love* 168

Cockney Alphabet, The 172

co-equal
'fatuous' 129

Coleridge, Samuel Taylor
on *talented*, 4; use of *soulmate*, 65; *phisiog* 185

collapse
transitive use stigmatised 50

Collins Complete Writing Guide
on *condone*, 19; *pristine* 20

Collins, V. H.
on *slip up*, 55; *ring up*, 58; *alright*, 78 fn; *all alone*, 79 fn; *unthinkable*, 136 fn; 'show words', 156; *gift*, *dire*, etc. 170–71

combining forms 76–77, 142

Comic English Grammar, The see Leigh, Percival

commeasurate
stigmatised 23–24

commence
'tasteless' 157–58, 160

compounds in general
40, 59, 61–66, 152, 165, *see also* reduplicative compounds

compounds formed with particles
67–72

condone
its meaning disputed 19–20

Conrad, Joseph
on 'meaningless' words 88

conversion
27–36; not restricted to nouns and verbs 31–35

Coverdale, Miles
use of *upside down* 22

Cowper, William
his 'pebbly' monosyllables 166–67

Craig, John
on *problematise* 109

critique
verb, a 'blemish' 29

Crowquill, Alfred (Alfred Henry Forrester)
use of *don'ted*, 47; on *artificial intestines, narrative*, 153; use of *U* 177

Cruikshank, George and Robert
use of *ickle* 90 fn

D

data
singular, stigmatised 143–144

decimate
its meaning disputed 139–41

De Quincey, Thomas
on 'aboriginal' English 163–64

deteriate
an ignorant 'scrap' 82–83

Dickens, Charles
use of *message* (verb), 30; *nutcracker* (verb), 35; *hang out*, 58; *old-fashioned*, 64; *wiglomeration*, 76; *tiddy ickle sing*, 90; knew Percival Leigh, 94 fn; friend of George Sala, 108; use of *ization*, 109; *centralization*, 109–10; accomplished in shorthand 180

diminutive suffixes
23, 91 fn, 97

disconnect
noun, 'to be reviled' 30

discourse analysis 86

disinterested
its meaning disputed 15, 79, 118–20

Disraeli, Benjamin
use of *monologize, paragraphise* 41

diss
'voguish' 31, 97 fn

Doctor Who
use of *wibbly-wobbly, dreamy-weamy*, etc. 95–96

Domesday Book, The
use of Latin abbreviations 174

donate
'abominable' 38

Donne, John
use of *disinterested*, 119; on *why* 165

double negatives 122–28

dove
for *dived*, stigmatised 48

Doyle, Sir Arthur Conan
use of *monumentous* 143

Dryden, John
use of *day-dream*, 65; on verse ruined by monosyllables 166

E

Economist Style Guide
on 'horrible words', 3, 5 fn; *enormity*, 13 fn; *pristine*, 20; *honeymoon period*, 25 fn; *critique* (verb), 29; 'adjectival reticules', 34; nouns as verbs, 35; phrasal verbs, 55; *upcoming, ongoing*, 68; *guesstimate*, 74; *wannabes*, 87; *finally*, 103; *disinterested*, 119; *pre-prepared, proactive*, etc., 129; *data* (singular), 144; *participate in, come up with*, 151; 'short words', 168; *likely* 169 fn

Egan, Pierce
on *bender* 113–14

Electric Telegraph of Fun, The
see Crowquill, Alfred

electrocution
'disgusting' 76

Eliot, George
use of *outlash, outleap*, etc., 69; *tchu, pst*, 85; *marls*, 86; *greenth, tumultuary*, etc., 99; *bigwiggism*, 108; terminal *not*, 114; *disbelief*, 115; on slang, 149; *pick*, 153; *commence*, 157; 'the odour of departed learning', 161; use of *phiz* 185

Eliot, T. S.
use of *enormity* 11–12

elocute
'ineffective' 39

enjoy
with unexpressed object, stigmatised 51

enormity
its meaning disputed 11–14

enthuse
'ignorant' 39

epicentre
for *centre*, stigmatised 130

Essay to Miss Catharine Jay, An
use of *D V 8, 40 tude*, etc. 180

etymological fallacy 19–21

etymology
18–21, *see also* folk etymology

F

fail
noun, stigmatised 30–31

false singulars and plurals 143–45

fancy language 155–62

Fielding, Henry
errors of Mrs Slipslop, 7; use of *rep*, 177; on *demirep* 177 fn

finally
its meaning disputed 103

finalise
'ungainly' 41

Fiske, Robert Hartwell
on *disconnect* (noun), 30; *elocute*, 39; *adaption*, 83–84; *orientate, preventative*, 84; *trepidatious*, 116; *disinterested*, 118; *ginormous, humongous*, 143 fn; monosyllables, 168–69; use of *likely* 169 fn

folk etymology 18–26

Fowler, Henry Watson
on *deteriate*, 83; 'genteelisms', *assist, proceed*, etc. 157

free elements 61 fn

frequentative suffixes 184

fund
    verb, a 'blemish' 28–29

G

gambit
    for *gamut* or *gauntlet*,
    stigmatised 16 fn

Garner, Bryan A.
    on 'not guilty' 118 fn

-gate
    'meaningless' 77

gent
    'pretentious' 177

genteelisms 157–58

Germanic English 120, 156, 158,
        163–64, 170, 183, 185

gift
    'genteel' 170; *see also* 'free gift' 134

Gilbert, W. S.
    use of *hang out* 58

ginormous
    'loathsome' 76–77, 142–43

gotten
    stigmatised 48

Gray, Thomas
    on false steps 'ne'er retrieved', 17;
    use of *vizzing, visiting
    about* 176

Gray's Anatomy
    use of *intestines, gut* 152

Griffith, Richard
    his wanton converting, 31, 35;
    use of *Namby Pambicks*, 95;
    old-fangled 117; his
    contribution to
    dictionaries 189

Griffith, Elizabeth
    on wanton converting, 31, 35–36;
    'privileged Dialect', 149, 169;
    enriching dictionaries 189

Grose, Francis
    on slipslops, 14 fn; *die hard*, 63;
    hums, hum box, 85; revised by
    Pierce Egan 113; on *binnacle words,
    word grubbers*, etc., 155, 159; '*C**t*' as
    'the monosyllable', euphemisms
    for, 166; *P.P.C., D. I. O.*, etc., 174;
    M. T. 176

guesstimate
    'horrible' 74–75

H

Hall, Fitzedward
    on *reliable* 100–101

halve
    intransitive use stigmatised 51

harbringer
    stigmatised 24–25

Hardy, Thomas
    use of *convexities, amplitudes* 106

Harris Academy, Upper Norwood
    on *like, extra*, etc. 153, 168 fn

Hazlitt, William
    on 'theatrical cadence', 155–56;
    'arbitrary pretension', 159; 'precise
    associations', 160; 'fine' words, 162;
    'familiar style' 182

Heffer, Simon
    on *prevaricate*, 11; *enormity*, 12;
    orphan, 18–20, 20; *pristine*, 20;
    miniscule, 23; nouns as verbs, 35;
    hung, 45; *collapse* (transitive), 50;
    halve, warn (intransitive), 50–51;
    sort, 59; *-gate*, 77; *alright*, 78;
    specialty, 83; *hopefully*, 103–104;

disinterested, 118–19; double negatives, 122–25; *decimation*, 139–40; vulgarity, 149–50; his use of forms he condemns, 150 fn; on 'tabloidese' 169–70

Henley, W. E.
use of *shouldn't wonder if we don't* 125

Henry VIII, king of England
use of *ducky* 91

Herbert, A. P.
on 'paper-sores', 4; Dr. Johnson's 'horrible' words, 29 fn; 'Ize-mania', 39, 42; *personalize*, 42; 'tail-twisters', 57; *knowledgeable*, 101–102; *television*, 120; *O.K.*, 181; *motivate*, *reactionary*, etc. 191

hiccough
'mere error' 22–23

High Society
on *pooped* 153

Hodgson, William B.
on 'our modern Blunderland' 190

Hooker, John
use of *a lot*, 142; his wasps 142, 145

hopefully
its meaning disputed 103–104

Hopkins, Gerard Manley
use of *spendsavour* 65

'horrible words' 3–5

Huddlestone, Rodney
on defining 'noun' 106 fn

Humphrys, John
on *step change*, 10 fn; nouns as verbs, 28; *rubbish*, *diss* (verbs), 31 fn; *progress*, *impact* (verbs), 36 fn; *anonymise*, 42; *enjoy*, 51; 'sprinkling prepositions', *stressed*

out, 55; *disinterested*, 119; *incredible*, 136 fn, 141 fn; sounding 'common', 149–50; 'grotesque abbreviations' 172–73, 176 fn, 180

humungous
'factitious' 143

hung
for *hanged*, stigmatised 45

Hunt, Leigh
on malapropisms and slipslops 9

I

idiom 16, 54–55, 57, 190

impact
verb, stigmatised 36 fn

imprecision 86, 138–45

inchoate
its meaning disputed 12

incredible
its meaning disputed 136, 141

infer
for *imply*, stigmatised 11

intransitive and transitive uses 50–53

irregardless
'illiterate' 126–28

-isms 108

'Ize-mania'
39–43, 111; two senses of *-ize* or *-ise*, 42; *-ise* French and *-ize* Greek 43

-ization
stigmatised 109–11

J
James, Henry
use of *ablutional* 110

jargon 3, 42

jeopardise
'intolerable' 40

Jerome, St.
use of *decimatis* 139

Johnson, Samuel
on *reckless*, 25–26; his 'horrible' words, 29 fn; on *jeopard*, 40; *womanise*, 43 fn; *irresistless*, *undisobliging*, 127–28; *phiz* 184–85

Jonson, Ben
use of *problematise* 40, 109

Joyce, James
use of *thunk*, 47; *smilesmirk*, 65; *uff*, 85; *weggebobble* 86

K
Kamm, Oliver
on *-gate*, 77; *alright*, *disinterested*, 79; *irregardless*, 127; *literally* 133 fn

Keats, John
use of *ruffy-tuffy* 94

kennings 63

King, Graham
on *condone*, 19; *pristine* 20

Kipling, Rudyard
use of *harumfrodite* 86–87

Koestler, Arthur
use of *wasm* 112

kudos
plural use stigmatised 144

L
Ladd, George Trumbull
use of *jeopard* 40

Lang, Andrew
How to Fail in Literature 1, 147

Larkin, Philip
use of monosyllables 168

Latimer, Hugh
use of *decimations* 139

Latinate English 19–21, 23–24, 31, 50, 56, 76, 82, 86, 99, 120, 139, 141, 143, 156–64, 168 fn, 170, 178 fn, 183–85

Lawson, Mark
use of *chartering* 14

lay
for *lie*, stigmatised 46

'leetspeak' or '1337SP34K' 179–80

Leigh, Percival
on infant 'comicalities', 94; defining 'noun', 105–106; use of *W up*, 177; on *gent*, 177; 'Mosaic dialect' 186 fn

Lewis, C. S.
on 'tactical definition', 18; use of *scientifiction*, 75; on 'verbicide', 136; *awfully*, *unthinkable* 136

Lewis, Matthew 'Monk'
errors of Mrs Slipslop 7

Lindisfarne Gospels
use of *fly* (noun) 27

like
'banned' 153

likely
for *probably*, stigmatised 169 fn

literally
figuratively 'intolerable' 133

litotes 122–27

loooooooool
stigmatised 179

M

macaronic English 182–87

malapropisms 9–11

'mangling' 86–88

Marlow, Christopher
on 'Che sera sera' 15

Marvell, Andrew
slated, 9; use of
new-fangled 117

merged words 77–79

metanalysis 79–81

Milne, A. A.
use of *hummy* 93

mischievious
stigmatised 84

Milton, John
use of *disturb* (noun), 30; *homefelt*,
awestruck, 65; *disobedience*, 113;
interpreted by Addison, 123; use of
horrent, *pontifice*, etc., 161; *displode*
186 fn

miniscule
'troublesome' 23

Mitford, Bertram
use of *trepidatious* 116

mitigate
for *militate*, stigmatised 11

monosyllables
163–71; their metrical quality
166–68

'monsters' 5, 112

Morgenbesser, Sidney
use of *yeah, yeah* 122 fn

morphemic pleonasm
129–32; *see also* 'pleonasm'

Muldoon, Paul
use of *conglomewrite* 75

mumbling 84–86

Murray, Lindley
on defining 'noun', 105; double
negatives 123–25

myriad
vague use stigmatised
138–39, 142

N

Nashe, Thomas
use of *-ize*, 40–41; *owl-light*,
windfucker, etc., 61–62, 165;
Prick-madame, 93; *footback*, 116;
on 'monasillables', 165; dog barks
'Saxon' 185

nauseous
its meaning disputed 102–103

Neal, Daniel
use of *decimated* 140

negative concord 32 fn, 124–28

negatives
48, 113–20, 133; *see also* 'double
negatives'

noisome
for *noisy*, stigmatised 20–21

non-lexical back channels 86

nonsense writing 69, 73, 88, 94

'non-words' 3, 77, 79, 86, 102, 142

nother
stigmatised 77, 79–81

nouns
verbed, and used attributively,
'horrible' 27–43, 67, 69, 169; *see also*
'abstract nouns'

-n't stigmatised 175 fn

O

o.k.
'imbecile' 181; *see also k, kk*, 172;
mkay 181

old-fangled
'puzzling' 117–18

ongoing
'horrible' 67–68

opposites 113–21

orientate
'cacophonic' 84

orphan
its meaning disputed 18–20

Orwell, George
use of *scientifiction*, 75; *ickle, ducky*,
etc. 90–91

Oxford English Dictionary
Victorian entries, 12 fn; on
hiccough, 23; *miniscule*, 23; *enthuse*,
39; *prioritise, pedestrianise*, 41;
lacking *otherise, amenitise*, etc., 42;
crap, 45; lacking *flag up, grass up*,
etc., 60; *weather-fend* and
land-damn undefined, 65; on
innards, 82; *ingram*, 87; *outright*,
97 fn; *verbicide*, 136 fn; *humungous*,
143; *bog*, 151, 182–83; *commence*,
157–58; *gent* 177

P

'paper-sores' 4

Parker, Dorothy
on *hummy*, 93; use of *fwowed*
47 fn, 93

particles
see 'phrasal verbs'; *see also*
'compounds formed with
particles'

'particular compounds'
see 'compounds formed with
particles'

passives 52 fn

past tense
contending forms, 44–49; *outgrabe*
irregular 69 fn

Pembroke, Mary Herbert
countess of
use of *upcheer* 68

personalize
'obscene' 42

phrasal verbs 54–60

phatic communion 86

Philips, Ambrose
'Namby Pamby' 95

plurals
false examples 143–45

pleonasm
79 fn; morphemic 129–32;
syntactic 134–36

portmanteau words 73–77, 93

Pope, Alexander
use of *Namby Pamby*, 95;
on 'modest Plainness', 155;
monosyllables 'stiff', 167;
'fantastic' words 182

prefixes
97; negative, 113–15, 118–19;
misidentified, 115–16 fn; used as
intensifiers, 129; *see also* 'affixes'

premise or *premisis*
for *premises*, stigmatised 144

pre-prepared
'just means *prepared*' 129

preventative
'no such word' 84

pristine
its meaning disputed 20

problematise
'what's that?', 40; 'not used' 109

progress
verb, stigmatised 36 fn

Provincial Medical Journal
on *rhypophagon,
antigropelos* 156

pseudo-antonyms 116

Pullum, Geoffrey K.
on defining 'noun' 106 fn

puns
8–9 fn, 16 fn, 27

Puttenham, George
on 'words monosillable' 164

R
recency illusion 29 fn

reduplicative babbling 94

reduplicative compounds 94–96

register
149–54; mismatches of
182–87

reliable
'ignorantly formed' 101–102

renumeration
stigmatised 23–25

repetition 133–34

restive
its meaning disputed 100, 102

rival opposites 118

Romilly, Joseph
use of *awful bad* 32 fn

Ruskin, John
on 'baby misbinefs',
92–93; his reduplicative
compounds 95 fn

S
sacreligious
stigmatised 23, 25

Sala, George
use of *clean-shirtedness,
chimney-pot-hattedness*, etc. 108

'Saxon' English
see 'Germanic English'

Scott, Sir Walter
book title mangled, 157 fn;
on slang 158

Screw magazine
on *fruit fly* 27 fn

Self, Will
on *inchoate*, 11–12; 'conservatives', 12
fn–13; use of *dimensionality*, 111; on
the 'banal middlebrow', 159; use of
fulguration, abulia, etc., 159–61; on
his use of 'the flowery', 183; use of
anguiform, wriggling, 183–84;
criticised for his prose style 186

semantic bleaching 133, 136

sentence adverbs 103

Shakespeare, William
errors of Dogberry, 9; use of *beach*,
19; *blanket* (verb), 28; *dialogue* (verb),
gust, (noun), etc., 30; *sluggardize*, 41;
conjure up, 56 fn; *bedroom, wormhole*,
63; *clotpole, dewdrop*, etc., 65;
understand, 69–70; *bubukle*, 74;
lonely, 78; *nuncle*, 80; *hoo*, 85;

Shakespeare, William – *cont.*
allicholly, argall, etc., 86; *lamkin,* 91
fn; *skimble skamble,* 94; *brainsickly,*
cannibally, 99; *concernancy,* 107;
infelicities of Holofernes, 108; use of
negatives, 113; *new-fangled,* 117;
negative concord, 125; *distain'd,*
undishonoured, 125–26; *loads,* 141–42;
Holofernes on 'verbosity', 156; use of
monosyllables, 167; on 'bastards and
syllables' 188

Shaw, George Bernard
use of *routine* (verb) 30

Shelley, Percy Bysshe
use of *shoplift,* 38; *-ism,* 108;
contrasting syllable-counts 167

Sheridan, Richard Brinsley
errors of Mrs Malaprop 9

shorthand
178; Dickens's use of 180

Sidney, Sir Philip
use of *womanise,* 42 fn; *fear-babes,*
navel-string, etc., 65; his sister 68

singulars
false examples 143–45

Sir Gawain and the Green Knight
on blushing 22

slang gangster, 31; military, 39;
displeasing, 55–56, 58; criminal,
63; forces, 76; church, 85; CIA,
119; 'of prigs', 149–50, 153; street,
155; 'thieves-Latin', 158;
oppressive, 160; 'nasty', 166;
monosyllabic, 170; gambling, 176;
'Anglo-Saxon', 183; 'buckish', 185

slipslops 7–17

Smith, Henry
use of *inbred* 70

Smith, Walter Chalmers
use of antonyms 113

snuck
stigmatised 48–49

sort
without *out,* an 'abomination' 59

Southey, Robert
use of *isms* 108

specialty
stigmatised 83

Steel, Richard
his desire for women readers, 35;
use of *voweled* 175–76

Stein, Gertrude
use of *precautious* 131

Steinbeck, John
on 'gangrened scholarship' 59–60

Sterne, Laurence
use of *not unkind-hearted*
123–24

stress out
'horrible' 55

suffixes
97; diminutive, 91 fn;
productive, 107 fn; frequentative,
184; *see also* 'affixes' and
'abstract nouns'

Surrey, Henry Howard,
earl of
use of *heaps* 141

Swift, Jonathan
on 'undeserving' words, 4–5; on
'Abhorrors', 16; use of *fair-sex*
(verb), 35; his 'little language',
sluttikins, etc., 92–93, 175; use of
up-a-dazy, 96; *anythingarian,* 99;
on 'fine Language', 161 fn;

monosyllables, 166; *do't, Phizz*, etc., 175–76, 184; 'daily Corruptions' of English, etc. 188

syncope 82–84

syntactic pleonasm
134–36; *see also* 'pleonasm'

T
'tabloidese' 169–70

'tactical definition' 18

talented
a 'barbarous vocable' 4 fn

tautology
see 'pleonasm'

Thackeray, William Makepeace
use of *h'm, pfui*, etc., 85; on Swift's 'little language' 93 transitive and intransitive uses 50–53

Trench, Richard Chenevix
on *shamefaced* 22 fn

trepidatious
'not a word' 116

Twain, Mark
on 'pleasurable disgust', 15; use of *yellocute*, 39; on *hogwash* as 'felicitous nomenclature', 183; *avalanche* (verb) 185

Tyndale, William
use of *busybody*, 61–62; *incomers* 71

U
U or *u*
for *you*, stigmatised, 172; *see also IOU*, 176; *like U best*, 177; *wuu2* 180

underwhelm
stigmatised 120, 130

un-dis 126–27

up
in phrasal verbs 55–58

V
'verbicide'
3 fn, 89, 136

'verbifying' 35–36, 65, 112

verbs
see in particular 'conversion', 'past tense', 'phrasal verbs', 'transitive and intransitive uses' and 'verbifying'

'vogue-words' 133 fn, 171

'voguish' 31 fn

W
Wallace, David Foster
his 'styleless' style reviewed, 52; use of *nother, snoot* 80

Walpole, Horace
his cat Selima, 17; use of *awaredom, gloomth*, etc., 100; *airgonation* 108

warn
intransitive use stigmatised 51

Wayne's World
use of terminal *not* 114

Wells, H. G.
use of *pitter-litter, wimble-wamble*, etc. 94–95

White, Richard Grant
on 'monsters', 5; 'usurpers', 7 fn; on *donate*, 38; *jeopardise*, 40; *preventative*, 84; *reliable*, 101; 'words that are not words' 189–90

Whitten, Wilfred and Whitaker, Frank
on *alright*, 78; *restive*, 100; Shakespeare's use of negative concord, 125; a *certain* amount, 138; suddenly fashionable words 182 fn

why
'damnable' 165

Wilson, Erin Cressida
use of *epicentre* 130 fn

Winn, Rev. Albert Curry
use of *condone* 19

word-class conversion
see 'conversion'

word inflation 129–37

Y
Yalden, Thomas
use of *fruition* 21

Young, Thomas
use of *anguiform* 184 fn

Z
Zwicky, Arnold
on the 'recency illusion' 29 fn